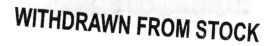

THE FOUNDATION OF THE NATIONAL GALLERY OF IRELAND

THE FOUNDATION OF
THE NATIONAL GALLERY OF IRELAND

CATHERINE DE COURCY

THE NATIONAL GALLERY OF IRELAND

British Library Cataloguing in Publication Data
de Courcy, Catherine
    The Foundation of the National Gallery
    of Ireland.
    1. National Gallery of Ireland — History
    I. Title   II. National Gallery of Ireland
    708.2'91835   N1250

    ISBN 0-903162-16-4

First published, 1985, by the National Gallery of Ireland,
Merrion Square West, Dublin 2.

Edited by Joanna Mitchel
Photography by Michael Olohan
Design, origination and print production by Printset & Design Ltd., Dublin

Printed in Ireland

CONTENTS

FOREWORD

The story of the foundation of the National Gallery of Ireland, as I have always known it, is a simple one. A group of public spirited people joined together in 1854 and decided to establish the Gallery. They had an Act of Parliament passed, raised money, built a gallery and bought a collection of pictures. While this might seem straightforward, it has always struck me that the establishment of the Gallery was rather too straightforward, and apart from that I have always been puzzled as to how this group of enthusiasts managed to act so quickly: it took a mere nine months or so to have the National Gallery of Ireland Act passed at Westminster.

Since the foundation of the Gallery in 1854 and its opening to the public ten years later, the Collection and the building have grown more than any of the founders could have imagined. On opening day there were about one hundred and forty paintings on show; to-day the collection numbers over two and a half thousand. In addition there is a collection of over five and a half thousand drawings and watercolours as well as prints and sculpture. The Gallery has had a varied history. In its first forty years the collection was formed. With a purchase grant of only £1,000 a year, great pictures such as Poussin's *Lamentation*, Rembrandt's *Rest on the Flight into Egypt* and Fra Angelico's *Attempted Martyrdom of SS. Cosmas and Damian* were purchased. But these were only three of many. Catalogues of the collection were published on a regular basis and the Gallery acquired the international reputation which it deserved. The hopes and aspirations of the founders were well fulfilled. At the beginning of this century the first substantial bequests and gifts were received through the Milltown Gift and the generosity of Sir Hugh Lane; and in 1903 the building was augmented by a new wing and doubled in size. But from about 1920 until the mid 1960's the Gallery's existence was more troubled: lack of funds and staff, and indeed public apathy, meant that it did not occupy the place in Irish life which it deserved. Since 1960, however, the National Gallery of Ireland has attained a new popularity and is today more appreciated than ever.

From previously unpublished material in the archive of the National Gallery Catherine de Courcy has been able to document the negotiations which led to the foundation of the Gallery. From letters and minute books she traces the intrigues involved in obtaining the site for the Gallery and the often fractious discussions over the architecture of the building. She has discovered the role played by no less a person than Benjamin Disraeli in obtaining extra funding for the building of the Gallery and she documents in detail the building itself which included such novelties as gas illumination and incorporated modern techniques of construction such as reinforced concrete.

In her research Catherine de Courcy has examined an enormous amount of previously unsifted material. In doing so she has completely rearranged and organised the Gallery archive so that it is now readily accessible to other scholars for research and she herself has written an account of the foundation of the National Gallery of Ireland that is as fascinating as it is exciting.

HOMAN POTTERTON
Director
National Gallery of Ireland
April 1985.

LIST OF ILLUSTRATIONS

ABBREVIATIONS

D.N.B.   Dictionary of National Biography

N.G.I.   National Gallery of Ireland

R.D.S.   Royal Dublin Society

R.H.A.   Royal Hibernian Academy

R.I.A.   Royal Irish Academy

R.I.A.I.   Royal Institute of the Architects of Ireland

R.I.I.   Royal Irish Institution

CHRONOLOGY

12th May 1853	Exhibition of Art and Art-Industry in Dublin is opened by the Earl of St. Germans.
14th July 1853	Dargan committee is launched in the Rotunda, Dublin.
31st October 1853	Exhibition closes.
1st November 1853	First meeting of the Irish Institution in Charlemont House.
4th January 1854	First annual exhibition of the Irish Institution opened at the R.H.A., Abbey Street.
20th July 1854	Viscount Canning introduces the National Gallery Bill in Parliament for its first reading.
10th August 1854	'An Act to provide for the Establishment of a National Gallery of Paintings, Sculpture and the Fine Arts, for the Care of a Public Library, and the Erection of a Public Museum in Dublin' passed in Parliament.
13th January 1855	First meeting of the Board of Governors and Guardians of the National Gallery, held at the R.H.A., Abbey Street.
31st July 1855	A grant of £6,000 voted in Parliament for the proposed National Gallery building.
5th November 1855	The Board of Governors and Guardians approve generally of George Mulvany's design.
4th March 1856	Jacob Owen prepares a report on Mulvany's design; it is not publicised.
7th March 1856	Foundation stone of National History Museum laid by the Earl of Carlisle.
24th March 1856	Mulvany's design approved by the Board of Marsh's library.
2nd April 1856	Mulvany's design approved by the Dargan Committee.
9th July 1856	Letter from Charles Lanyon to Richard Griffith; first suggestion of Lanyon's involvement in the National Gallery.
17th July 1856	William Lynn attends Board meeting to present Lanyon's plans.
21st August 1856	Richard Griffith is ordered by the Board to get 'matured plans' from Charles Lanyon.
9th February 1857	Lanyon's design adopted by the Board of Governors and Guardians on the understanding that it was to be constructed in two phases as outlined by Richard Griffith.

20th April 1857	Building Trustees present report on tenders received for the construction of the building to the Board of Governors and Guardians. Contractors, Cockburn and Son, estimate that Lanyon's building would cost £23,000.
20th April 1857	Memorial on behalf of the building trustees sent to the Lords of the Treasury seeking a substantial increase in the building grant.
26th August 1857	Treasury official replies to memorial of the 20th April refusing to sanction an additional grant.
31st August 1857	National History Museum inaugurated with public lecture delivered by Dr. David Livingstone.
5th December 1857	Adoption of Lanyon's plans of the 9th February rescinded.
9th December 1857	George Mulvany writes to Treasury on behalf of the Board requesting Treasury to reconsider refusal of the 26th August 1857.
17th December 1857	Treasury official repeats his refusal of the 26th August.
6th February 1858	New plans by Lanyon adopted by Board.
19th February 1858	In Parliament Lord Palmerston's liberal party is replaced by an unstable government led by Lord Derby.
May 1858	Francis Fowke visits Dublin to investigate the delay in the construction of the National Gallery.
24th June 1858	Benjamin Disraeli, Chancellor of the Exchequer, promises the Irish Institution a larger grant for the building.
22nd September 1858	Francis Fowke presents his report on the National Gallery building to The Marquis of Salisbury, Chairman of the Committee of the Council on Education in the Department of Science and Art.
1st October 1858	The Board of Governors and Guardians of the National Gallery adopt Fowke's report.
13th January 1859	Richard Griffith, on behalf of the building trustees enters into an agreement with Cockburn & Son for excavation, drainage, and entire mason work of the exterior of the building.
29th January 1859	The Earl of Eglinton lays the first stone of the Gallery on Leinster Lawn.
6th September 1862	George Mulvany appointed the first Director of the National Gallery.
4th October 1862	The Board of Governors and Guardians holds its first meeting in the new National Gallery building.
30th January 1864	The National Gallery is formally opened by The Earl of Carlisle.

CHAPTER I

Concept 1853-1854

Introduction

The National Gallery of Ireland opened its doors to the public in 1864 following an inauguration ceremony presided over by the Lord Lieutenant, the Earl of Carlisle. The small collection of paintings, drawings, watercolours sculpture contained few works of importance but was recognised as the nucleus of a national collection which would be developed by successive administrations. In 1864, however, it was the building which stood as the symbol of the permanent position of the fine arts in Ireland. The solid purpose-built structure had been the focus of the National Gallery project since its initiation in 1853, and the success or failure of the entire plan had depended on matters concerning it rather than those concerning the collection. Over the years the progress of the building was hampered by problems arising from local conflicts of interest, inadequate finance, interference from the civil service and uncooperative governments, all of which threatened to halt the scheme before the first stone was laid in 1859.

The history of the building is well documented in the National Gallery archive,[1] largely thanks to the foresight of the Under-Secretary at the time, Col. Thomas A. Larcom, who collated relevant material from his records and deposited it in the Gallery. Examination of the archive has revealed the extraordinary patience and energy with which the complications of the new institution were dealt with and successfully overcome by a small group of men, some of whom were already greatly occupied with the aftermath of revolution and famine in the country. The development of the building when traced through the archive lends itself to three chronological subdivisions thus: part I deals with the period between the initiation of the project in 1853 and the Act of Parliament in August 1854, and looks at the background to the clauses which were to influence the progress of the building; part II, from 1854 to the start of the construction in 1859, follows the difficulties, caused largely by the Act, in acquiring a suitable design and adequate finance; and part III, from 1859 to the inauguration ceremony in 1864 looks specifically at the design of the building which was novel in methods of construction and lighting; it concludes with the opening ceremony and the enthusiastic press reaction to the long-awaited establishment of a National Gallery of Ireland.

2

The Dublin Exhibition of 1853

In 1853 a large exhibition of Irish industry was held in a temporary glass and iron structure on Leinster Lawn, overlooking Merrion Square. Such industrial exhibitions had steadily increased in popularity since the first of its kind was held in London in 1756 at which the Society of Arts had offered prizes for excellence in manufacturing industry, and had subsequently exhibited the works entered for competition. More recently the celebrated Crystal Palace exhibition had opened in London in 1851, and in 1853 Cork had hosted a similar event on a smaller scale. The Dublin exhibition developed the concept further by devoting almost one third of the vast exhibition area to a display of the fine arts borrowed from Prussia, France, the Netherlands and Belgium as well as from Britain and Ireland. In the introduction to the catalogue the organisers claimed this innovation as '... the first instance of the association of Art, that is the Ideal, with Material Industry ...'[2] (illus 1).

The philanthropic zeal of the exhibition's organisers did not go unrewarded. The citizens of Dublin flocked to Merrion Square, many returning frequently; the door receipts recorded almost one million visitors between May and October. The fine arts section was tremendously popular, attracting a great deal of popular acclaim. Some of those closely connected to this part of the exhibition saw the opportunity to harness public enthusiasm and use it to establish a permanent exhibition of the fine arts in Ireland, on the model of provincial galleries in France which were built by local subscription, and in Britain most notably the National Gallery of Scotland which was under discussion at the time and was likely to receive substantial Government aid.[3]

The Irish Institution

John Pigot (1822-1871), a lawyer and son of the Lord Chief Baron, David Pigot, wrote a memorandum towards the end of the 1853 in which he proposed a plan to establish a National Gallery of Ireland. The memorandum was quite detailed with regard to sources of finance for such a project, as well as administrative and legal matters. It was discussed amongst those most actively involved in the fine arts section, most notably the Lord Chancellor, Maziere Brady. On the basis of their informal discussions, which were held in David Pigot's Dublin residence, a formal meeting was held on the 1st November in Charlemont House, Parnell Square. The group at this meeting, consisting of ten people closely associated with Dublin cultural life, adopted the name 'The Irish Institution' and recorded as their sole objective 'The promotion of Art in Ireland by the formation of a permanent Exhibition in Dublin and eventually of an Irish National Gallery'[4] (illus 2 and 3 and 4).

1. Visit of Queen Victoria to the Industrial Exhibition 1853 by James Mahony. N.G.I., cat. no. 2453.

3

They lost little time in organising their forthcoming campaign. Lord Talbot de Malahide, Chairman of the Fine Arts Committee, was appointed treasurer; George Mulvany R.H.A. and J. Calvert Stronge, were appointed secretaries and the Earl of Charlemont, was elected president in his absence. Eight vice-presidents were chosen from the distinguished list of gentlemen who had pledged support for the project. Confident that they would achieve their objective without the intervention of Government aid; the founders of the Irish Institution designed their campaign carefully in order to maintain popular interest until the Gallery was completed (illus 5 and 6 and 7).

The plan they adopted was twofold. Firstly, 'to educate public taste', a loan exhibition would be held annually for as long as was necessary, the first one to

2. *David Pigot, Lord Chief Baron (1797-1873) published in the Dublin University Magazine 1874. Reproduced by kind permission of the Board of Trinity College Dublin.*

3. *Sir Maziere Brady, Lord Chancellor (1796-1871) by Thomas Jones. N.G.I., cat no. 132.*

4. Charlemont House by James Malton. Reproduced by kind permission of the National Library of Ireland.

be organised immediately by asking lenders to the Industrial Exhibition to leave their works of art in Dublin for an extended period. A small entrance fee would defray any expense. Secondly, the public would be invited to become members of the Institution at an annual subscription rate of one guinea for men, 10/6d for women. This would not only finance the administration of the Institution but would also give people a personal interest in the progress of the Gallery. They agreed that donations of works of art and of money for the permanent collection would be accepted but no concerted effort was to be made in that direction for the time being.

On the 4th November they issued a lengthy statement announcing the formation of the Irish Institution and the course they intended to take towards achieving their objective. They published detailed figures of how much money would be required and how it would be used for maximum effect. Members of the institution and all subscribers would be entitled to free access to the forthcoming exhibition as would donors of works of art or money.

The public response to both of the schemes was overwhelming. When an enlarged committee met two weeks later, decisions had to be made as to how to control both the number of loan exhibits and the number of members. With regard to the proposed exhibition the secretaries reported that 'in almost every instance (they had) met with generous cooperation on the part of the

proprietors of the various works recently placed in the Great Exhibition'. So it was agreed that the artists on the committee would select the most suitable works for exhibition, 'bearing in mind that only works of really high merit and authenticity could be accepted'. The secretaries also informed the general committee that both the Royal Hibernian Academy and the Royal Dublin Society had offered storage facilities, the former also offering to host the Institution's exhibition in its rooms in Lower Abbey Street.

The committee then went on to discuss 'the propriety of limiting the number of the committee or of regulating future admission'; no reasons were given as to why they wanted to curtail membership but it may have been related to the fact that all members were eligible to attend meetings, and if the

5. *Lord Talbot de Malahide (1805-1883) by Frederick Sargent. Reproduced by kind permission of the Trustees of the National Portrait Gallery, London.*

6. *George Mulvany (1809-1869) self-portrait. N.G.I., cat. no. 926.*

6

7. *Francis William Caulfield,
2nd Earl of Charlemont, Lord
Lieutenant (1775-1863) by
Thomas Lawrence. N.G.I.,
cat. no. 379.*

committee became very large it would become increasingly difficult to conduct business effectively. It was decided that henceforth candidates would have to be proposed by three members of the committee at least a week before selection day, and then be subject to a ballot 'one black bean in four to exclude'.

Thus within two weeks the Irish Institution became firmly established in the public eye, and with it the idea of a National Gallery of Ireland. But if the long-term plan was to be successful a great deal of less attractive work had to be done, particularly in relation to the building. The founders of the Institution realised that a collection would take many years to develop and to put their energies into that rather than into the building would be non-productive in the long-run. So the men who had undertaken the project in the first place now concentrated on the planning and organisation of the building.

Proposal for a building

On the 17th November the finance sub-committee presented a detailed report on the subject of the building to the general committee. It contained information about the amount of money required to construct a suitable building, how the money should be acquired and managed, and where the Gallery should be located. Although they stressed that the report was provisional, pointing out that it should soon be the responsibility of a building committee, they had prepared it with such care, and presented it with such confidence that it was unlikely that any future committee would alter their findings considerably.

The report suggested at the outset that a building committee should be appointed. It recommended that the new committee should consist of twelve members of the general committee, the secretaries, and three building trustees. The latter were to be selected from the annual subscribers, and ownership of the site and the building was to be vested in them until such time as the building could be handed over to a National Gallery Board. The report further recommended that the money for the building should be raised by shares of £25 each, with a maximum annual interest of 5% and should remain separate from any other fund raised by the Institution. It stated that £5,000 would be sufficient to construct a plain building in which ∴ every species of external architectural ornament shall be, for the present, altogether dispensed with …'.

Selection of a site

The sub-committee had also thoroughly investigated possible sites. The essential requirements for a suitable site were firstly that it should be large enough not only to accommodate a building at least three hundred feet long, and sixty feet wide, but should also have enough space to permit future expansion, and secondly that it should be in an area accessible to the public and worthy of housing a national collection. Four sites were brought to the general committee's attention. The first one was a plot of land on Park Street (now Lincoln Place). This, it was noted, would have been an accessible location but there were houses adjacent to the site which would have prohibited future expansion. The second site to be considered was on Clonmel Square, south of St. Stephen's Green. In 1865 the temporary buildings for the Industrial Exhibition were to be constructed here but although it had 'Abundance of space…good air… good … light' it was considered too far from the city as a location for the National Gallery. A third possibility was the building formerly occupied by the Royal Irish Institution. This building, in College Street, would have been convenient as it was ready for immediate occupation, but in the long

8. *Royal Irish Institution, College Street (demolished 1866). Reproduced by kind permission of the Allied Irish Bank.*

term it would have serious limiting disadvantages. The committee, however, was determined that the fourth site would prove the most favourable, and this was the site of the 1853 Industrial Exhibition, the north side of Leinster Lawn (Illus 8).

Leinster Lawn, the land between Leinster House and Merrion Square was owned by Sir Sidney Herbert M.P. (1810-1861), step-brother and heir presumptive to the 12th Earl of Pembroke.[5] He had been supportive to the organisers of the Industrial Exhibition, providing them with accommodation in his house on upper Merrion Street. Thus he would have been a familiar figure to most of the members of the Institution's sub-committee who approached him informally to ascertain whether he would be willing to allow a permanent exhibition hall to be built on his land. He responded to their request most agreeably, assuring them that they had his permission if they could make

9. *Sidney Herbert, 1st Baron of Lea (1810-1861), by Sir Francis Grant. Reproduced by kind permission of the Trustees of the National Portrait Gallery, London.*

suitable arrangements with his present tenants, the Royal Dublin Society. The Society, which owned Leinster House and the land west of it, held the Lawn on a long-term lease, (illus 9).

The conclusion of the finance sub-committee's report to the general committee on the building strongly indicates that informal conversations had been going on between members of the Society and those of the Institution prior to its compilation. It stated: 'Your committee are of the opinion that no site could be found in Dublin more favourable to the purposes of the Institution that a portion of that Lawn ...'. The complete findings were then handed over to a newly selected committee which would be responsible for securing the site legally and organising the finance.

The Building Committee's first step was to make the arrangements necessary to acquire the site. Following its first meeting on the 3rd December a deputation led by Talbot de Malahide and including John Pigot, Mulvany and Stronge, prepared 'to communicate the desire of the committee to enter into arrangements with the Dublin Society with a view to the erection of a gallery on the north side of Leinster Lawn.' Preliminary discussions took place on the 8th December when the group attended a Society council meeting. They presented a general outline of the plan which, they recorded, was received 'in the most friendly manner'. The council agreed to recommend the plan to its general committee which was due to meet on the 12th January 1854.[6]

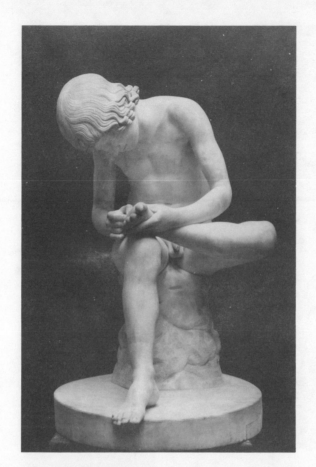

10. *'Boy extracting thorn' by Giacomo Vanelli. N.G.I., cat. no. 8085. Presented by Mrs Carmichael to the Irish Institution for the National Gallery Collection in 1854.*

First annual exhibition

The rapid development of the Irish Institution during the five weeks between the Society's meetings gives us an indication of the level of preparation which must have gone on prior to its formation in November. The first annual exhibition opened on the 4th January 1854 in the R.H.A. rooms. Over 160 items were on view of which two marble sculptures and three paintings now belonged to the permanent national collection. The picture fund stood at £200, none of which had been solicited formally. More significant, however, was an offer of £5,000 to be spent on a building, the exact amount of money that the building committee had hoped to raise in shares. The offer came from another committee formed as a result of the Industrial Exhibition — 'The Dargan Committee' — established to honour William Dargan, the man who had been largely responsible for the success of the Exhibition[7] (illus 10 and 11).

11

11. *William Dargan by Stephen Catterson Smith. N.G.I., cat. no. 141. Fragment of a picture painted 1862 for the Dargan Committee.*

William Dargan

In 1852 William Dargan (1799-1867), who had made a considerable fortune constructing railways, had presented the R.D.S. with an ambitious plan. He had suggested that its forthcoming triennial Exhibition in 1853 should be greatly expanded to emulate the exhibitions held recently in Paris, London and Cork. Dargan initially lent £20,000 to the R.D.S. towards the cost of the exhibition on certain conditions. These included the right to nominate the senior officials of the committee responsible for organising the exhibition. He further promised to forward any additional finance on the same conditions. He asked that the money would be refunded to him at 5% interest from the proceeds of the Exhibition. By the time the Exhibition closed Dargan had forwarded £87,000 of which he had little hope of receiving more than £60,000 in repayment.

The Dargan Committee

The 'Dargan Committee' was formed in July 1853, shortly after the opening of the Great Exhibition. A request, signed by nearly two thousand people including peers, archbishops, members of Parliament, judges and municipal representatives was sent to the Lord Mayor of Dublin, Robert Henry Kinahan, asking for a public meeting to consider 'the best means of rendering a tribute of respect and gratitude to our Fellow Countryman William Dargan Esq. for his unparalleled exertions, which under the blessing of Almighty God have so singally tended to benefit our Country by developing her resources and directing the Industry of her people.' The Lord Mayor willingly agreed to preside over a meeting to be held in the Rotunda on the 14th July 1853. It was decided at that meeting that Dargan's name should be perpetuated in some way that would be 'permanently useful in extending Industrial Education'. A fund was established, and subscriptions of anything from a shilling upwards were accepted. A vast committee was appointed and included anyone who had signed the requisition, anyone who was present, as well as many who wanted to join but had not done either. Among the fifty or so named in the first address of the so called 'Dargan Committee' were three founder members of the Irish Institution. Four trustees were chosen from the committee to administer the fund; the Lord Mayor, Edward McDonnell who was the Lord Mayor elect, Joseph Boyce and James Perry. The chairman of the Industrial Exhibition, Mr. George Roe (1795-1875) who was of course chosen for that job by William Dargan, was appointed chairman of the 'Dargan Committee' and Lord Talbot de Malahide (1805-1883) was appointed honorary treasurer. By the 1st November 1853, over £5,000 had been collected.

In an address to the public, published by the Dargan Committee on the 9th January 1854, it was announced 'that it is the opinion of the Committee that the best way of applying the funds placed at its disposal, ... will be by erecting a suitable building for the reception and exhibition of works for the fine arts, and their applications to Industry, to be called 'The Dargan Institute'.

It would appear that no formal conference took place between the Dargan Committee and the Irish Institution, and that the former felt it unnecessary to set any conditions for transferring the fund at this stage. As a result when the matter of conditions did arise between the Dargan Committee and the Institution's successors, the then newly established National Gallery Board, in 1856, there was conflict. The former assumed that Dargan's name would be placed over the principal entrance door, but the Gallery Board adamantly refused to comply, insisting that it was under no obligation to do so. A compromise was reached and the following conditions were those finally agreed upon: that a bust of Dargan, presented to the Dargan Committee by

12. *The Dargan Memorial Tablet on the east elevation of the National Gallery.*

the Earl of Clancarty, should be placed either in the entrance hall or on the principal staircase; that the largest hall of the intended building should be called the 'Dargan Hall', and that his dedication should be a matter of conspicuous and permanent inscription; that a portrait of Dargan, then being painted by Catterson Smith, should be hung, equally conspicuously, in one of the picture galleries; and that a lengthy inscription, composed by the Committee, should be placed on a tablet outside the building. In the long run, the influence of the Dargan Committee having waned, these conditions were not fully observed: the bust and portrait of Dargan were not afforded particular pre-eminence, the largest hall never became known as the 'Dargan Hall' and no inscription was placed therein. The tablet, however, its inscription somewhat shortened, was incorporated into the eastern elevation. As if in compensation for these shortcomings a large bronze statue of Dargan, paid for by the Dargan Committee and executed by Thomas Farrell, was placed on the lawn in front of the Gallery (illus 12).

First plans for the site

Such conflict, however, was not anticipated by either group when the offer was received by the Irish Institution's building committee and gratefully

13. Photograph of Leinster Lawn, c.1900. Lawrence Collection, National Library of Ireland.

accepted in January 1854. The committee, now secure in the knowledge that adequate finance for the building was available, could proceed with confidence into making arrangements about the site. The R.D.S. general committee met on the 12th January 1854 and discussed a ground plan of Leinster Lawn which included the proposed National Gallery. The proposal which emerged from this meeting serves as a further indication of the support with which the founders of the Institution had undertaken the task.

The plan in question depicted two oblong buildings adjoining Leinster House at right angles, as if forming wings to the house. The intention was that their elevations facing the lawn would be symmetrical. The proposed National Gallery was to be in the building on the northern side of the lawn, and a museum of Natural History on the southern side. A large area of lawn was to be maintained between the buildings as a garden for the R.D.S. For many years the Society had been planning to provide suitable accommodation for its growing natural history collection and indeed had been considering a proposal to build a museum on the Kildare Street side of Leinster House (illus 13).

This attractive idea of blending two new buildings in with the old house was probably devised by Sir Richard Griffith (1784-1878), the chairman of the Board of Works, and Frederick Clarendon, an architect employed by the Board

14. *Richard Griffith by Thomas Farrell. Published in:* 'Richard Griffith, 1784-1878': Royal Dublin Society Historical Studies in Irish Science and Technology. *Reproduced by kind permission of the Royal Dublin Society.*

who was, at that time, working on a design for the Museum. The Museum was to be built with public funds and consequently the Board of Works was obliged to have some part in the construction of the southern building although it was not necessary to employ one of its staff to design it. There was no question at this stage of the Irish Institution receiving public funds for the National Gallery. However, because there was to be a relationship between the design of the gallery and that of the museum the Institution was in the fortunate position of working with a man of Griffith's calibre and expertise from the outset of the project. He had built up a considerable reputation during his lengthy and diverse career and his personal dynamism was to have a significant influence on the progress of the Gallery building during the coming years[8] (illus 14).

There is no record in the archive to suggest that the R.D.S. contacted the Institution to relay the result of its meeting of the 12th January. Nevertheless some sort of communication must have been established for each body then proceeded to make its own arrangements with Sidney Herbert's solicitor, John E. Vernon, presumably assuming cooperation of the other bodies in the plan as proposed.

16

The Parliamentary Bill

For the Institution the major complication of building a permanent structure on Herbert's land required that an Act of Parliament be passed to sanction a lease in perpetuity. There was other reasons for seeking an Act of Parliament, not least of which was to constitute the new venture as the National Gallery of Ireland. The following months saw a major effort on the part of a small group of men to draft a suitable Bill and have it read and passed before the end of the current Parliamentary session in August 1854.[9]

John Pigot, one of the founders of the Institution, and a solicitor by profession, drafted the Bill. In this he was advised by his father David Pigot, the Lord Chief Baron (1797-1873) and by the Lord Chancellor, Maziere Brady. Both of these senior legal figures were members of the Institution, although David Pigot seldom attended the meetings. Two senior government officials were also involved from the early stages of the Bill; these were the Chief Secretary Sir John Young, and his permanent Under-Secretary Colonel Thomas Larcom. It is difficult to ascertain the names of other members of the Institution who might have assisted with the Bill. What seems certain however, is that John Pigot and his confidantes deliberately wished to keep the matter within a small circle. The secretaries, Mulvany and Stronge, were informed of its progress regularly but only after debate on the widsom of taking them into counsel and even then, only when it proved expedient.

The Chief Secretary for Ireland at the time, Sir John Young (1807-1876) spent most of his term of office living in London. In a letter written in June 1854 he had pledged to do 'all in my power' to facilitate the smooth passage of the Bill through Parliament. He made all the necessary arrangements to have the Bill read, firstly in the House of Lords, and then in the House of Commons. Drafts of the Bill were sent to him for approval, and he frequently made some changes in the wording and content, possibly with advice from Irish M.P.s resident in London[10] (illus 15).

The Government offical who, in fact, did most of the work on the Bill was Colonel Thomas Larcom, the Under-Secretary (1801-1879). Permanently resident in Ireland his duty was to keep the Chief Secretary informed of the daily affairs in the Country. He was kept constantly informed of the developments on the Bill by the Institution's *ad hoc* committee, and while the could have had a considerable influence on its content, being the liaison between Dublin and London, he preferred to advise and inform, seldom expressing a personal opinion. Nevertheless Larcom was to play a significant part in the early history of the Gallery. An engineer by profession, he had been working in Ireland for many years, and had been deputy chairman of the Board of Works before his appointment to the position of Under-Secretary in 1853.

17

With Richard Griffith, he was to handle and resolve many of the difficulties the National Gallery building committee encountered during the following years before the building was finally completed in 1864 (illus. 16).

Arrangement for a lease

The first area of the Bill to be worked on related to ownership of the site. Sidney Herbert's lease for Leinster Lawn was limited to one hundred and eighty years; a permanent institution would require a lease in perpetuity and this could only be obtained by an Act of Parliament. The Institution's *ad hoc* committee was anxious to lease the relevant portion of the lawn directly from Herbert; any reference to the R.D.S. in the Bill would necessitate further talks with the Society and this, David Pigot pointed out, would cause 'great delay'.

15. *John Young by J. Holmes.*
Reproduced by kind permission of the Royal Ontario Museum.

16. *Col. Thomas A. Larcom by Christopher Moore.*
Reproduced by kind permission of the Ordance Survey, Phoenix Park.

So John Pigot prepared a clause which met with the provisions of the 'Leasing Powers Bill' being processed by Parliament at the time.[11] Such a clause would empower National Gallery representatives to lease the site directly from Herbert without the involvement of a third party.

Board of Governors and Guardians

The next step was to decide on the format of the National Gallery representation in which the land would be vested. It was agreed that building trustees should be appointed and that they should have ownership of the site until the building was completed. On completion, ownership of the building and the site would transfer to a Board of Governors and Guardians, which would also be responsible for the administration of the Gallery. The Institution's finance committee had originally suggested that there should be three trustees but on John Pigot's recommendation the number was increased to five with the inclusion of two members of the Dargan Committee. His reason for making such a recommendation was understandable; he explained in a letter to Larcom: 'if the chairman... and another active member of their body be of the five trustees (the Dargan Committee) will not fail to feel confidence in placing their funds in such hands'. Thus George Roe and Thomas Hutton were named trustees of the Gallery. The growing possibility of receiving Government assistance, for reasons which will emerge shortly, made the Chairman of the Board of Works, Richard Griffith, another obvious choice for inclusion among the trustees. Thomas Larcom and the President of the Irish Institution, the Earl of Charlemont, also agreed to act as trustees (illus 17).

The building trustees were to be empowered to lease the site, and to administer all monies received in connection with the construction of the Gallery. On completion they would disband, turning it and its contents over to the Board of Governors and Guardians.

The Board, as envisaged by the *ad hoc* committee, would consist of fifteen members because, John Pigot noted, '...it appears to present a convenient middle term for an efficient committee.' It was to be made up of a mixture of *ex-officio* members — the presidents of the R.H.A. and the R.I.A., and the Chairman of the Board of Works: and of elected representatives — two of the R.H.A., three of the Lord Lieutenant, and seven elected by donors to the Gallery of either two guineas or a work of art worth £20 or more. The donors' representatives had to be selected by a body of at least one hundred; if the number of donors fell below one hundred the Lord Lieutenant was empowered to select persons to fill the vacancies that occurred on the Board. Representatives were to be elected for a term of five years.

19

The presence of the donors' representatives on the Board was central to the long term plan for the Gallery. John Pigot explained '…most annual subscribers will be either wholly or in part attracted by the privilege of admission in return for subscription…whereas the chief objects of such an institution, as an educational one, demand that it should be open free of any charge…it is proposed to encourage this source of support by conferring upon such subscribers and upon substantial donors of money or of works of art, the right of electing Governors of the National Gallery and of electing a considerable proportion of these since it is neither desirable nor required that the Government should possess any very extensive power of nomination to that Board'. (Only one such election ever took place, and that was in 1869, five years after the Gallery opened.) The Chairman of the Board of Works as an *ex-officio* member was regarded as important to facilitate easy communication between the Board and the National Gallery on the assumption that the former would maintain and improve the building after its completion.

The *ad hoc* committee did not feel it necessary to develop the administration of the Gallery further for the purposes of the Act. The matter was not discussed formally at Irish Institution committee meetings, and there is no evidence to suggest that it was discussed informally with anyone other than those already mentioned. There can be no doubt but that the structure and content of the Bill merited discussion if only to ensure that there would be no dissatisfaction on any side when it eventually became public. In fact it would seem that it was the potential for dissatisfaction which promoted the inner circle to keep the preparation of the Bill amongst themselves.

Proposal for a Public Library

An elaborate plot was developing in relation to the National Gallery project which required that there should be a minimum time lapse between the publication of the Bill and its enactment in Parliament. This plot concerned the move to establish a public library in Dublin.

In the mid-19th century Dublin boasted some fine libraries: the R.I.A., Trinity College, King's Inn, R.D.S. and Archbishop Marsh's Library. Although learned members of Dublin society would have experienced little difficulty in gaining access to most of these libraries none of them was completely accessible to the growing number of literate people among the lower and middle classes. An unsigned article published in the *Journal of Social Progress* in March 1853 explained the need: '…in every country where a considerable number of the inhabitants know how to read, Public Libraries will continue to be a necessity until immense improvements in printing, and a complete revolution in the publishing trade, shall have brought the more valuable productions of literature and science…within the reach of the poorer and working classes of the community'. The author concludes the article with a note drawing the readers attention to the National Gallery project and the possibility of devoting the ground floor of the new building to a public library. Five years earlier, in response to the successful opening of the British Museum, the Gallery at Hampton Court and the National Gallery (London) to the public, a select committee had investigated the possiblity of establishing public libraries in Great Britain and Ireland. Amongst those invited to submit evidence to the committee in Ireland was Edward Purefoy Colles, a member of the R.D.S. library committee and its first chairman. From his evidence it is clear that Colles was anxious that the Society's library should form the nucleus of the first public library: in answer to a question, number 2927, as to what the best mode of establishing a large public library in Dublin might be, he stated: 'I think the best germ of it would be the library of the Dublin Society; then, asked as to whether he would combine it with another existing library he replied 'By no manner of means; I think that should be guarded against' adding 'The rivalry between three or four libraries existing at Dublin, and the superiority of some in particular departments, has stimulated others to exertion and has produced great improvements'; he further noted that the most suitable location for a library would be a fashionable rather than a central area, and Leinster House was undoubtedly in a fashionable area.[12]

Marsh's Library

The Irish Institution's founding fathers, most notably David Pigot, now intended to include the National Gallery project in this cultural struggle. Pigot wrote numerous letters to Thomas Larcom in which his plan for a public library developed gradually. The focus of his attention was Archbishop Marsh's library, St. Patrick's Close. Marsh's library had been established by an Act of Parliament in 1707 and, of all the libraries in the city it had the largest potential readership being open to 'all graduates and gentlemen'. However, in recent years it had become somewhat neglected and the building, situated adjacent to a pharmaceutical factory, was in a poor state of repair and in constant danger of being destroyed by fire. It was now suggested that the problem of neglect could be solved by transferring the collection of books to Merrion Square, a move which would require another Act of Parliament[13] (illus 18).

It would appear that the association of Marsh's library with the National Gallery project was prompted initially by the existence of the Dargan Fund. In November 1853 Sir John Young wrote to George Roe, Chairman of the Dargan Committee, suggesting that the money might be used to rehouse the Marsh Collection in a new building; Roe replied that he would put it to the committee but added that he thought it likely that the Irish Institution would receive the fund. However, it would seem that the inner circle of the Institution already had plans for the library. John Pigot's memorandum written in 1853 had suggested that advantage might be taken of the proposed National Gallery project 'to provide for a tolerably complete public library in Dublin by making that of the Royal Dublin Society auxiliary to Marsh's. But in order to include provision for such an arrangement in the draft bill now it would have been necessary to consult the R.D.S. and this they were most reluctant to do. To avoid involving the Society David Pigot devised a series of clauses which would provide the parliamentary means to transfer the library, change its administrative structure and permit amalgamation with another library without commitment on any part.

He explained the need and the method in his correspondence to Larcom. On the integration of Marsh's collection with another he wrote 'It is of the

18. *Marsh's Library. Published in* 'All Graduates and Gentlemen' *by M. McCarthy. Reproduced by kind permission of the Board of Governors and Guardians of Marsh's Library.*

greatest importance to have, at last, a good miscellaneous library, accessible to the public at large. Marsh's Library, though a valuable collection and comprising a good deal of English Literature up to the middle of the last century, is very deficient in modern books. Of these there is a good collection in the library of the Dublin Society...let provision be introduced into the Act of Parliament...that it is expedient to allow to the Dublin Society the option, and to give them the power of uniting their collection of books to that in Marsh's Library... whenever they shall desire to do so...; (it should be remembered that the National Library of Ireland was not established until 1877); and on the library administration he mused 'it occurs to me that great objection may hereafter be made to the governors of Marsh's Library being the permanent trustees of a great public library. They consist of four ecclesiastics and four lawyers. And with the most profound respect for both professions, I think they ought not to be the exclusive directors and guardians

23

of literature'. He further suggested that after moving the collection to Merrion Square the old building in St. Patrick's Close would be sold and the proceeds used to purchase a house in the vicinity of the new building for the resident librarian. He proposed that although the library and the gallery would be housed in the same building each was to have exclusive control over that section of the building that it occupied, separate entrances would be installed with no direct public access between them.

There would certainly have been some advantages for the National Gallery project in drawing Marsh's Library into the plans, particularly with regard to finances; John Young noted that as the Library was maintained by public funds he could ask the Lord Lieutenant to seek a grant for the new building from the Government, adding that he thought it likely that the Institution would receive at least £5,000 in view of the generous grants recently given to the National Gallery of Scotland. But whatever the reasons for including Marsh's library in the plans for the National Gallery, or indeed including the National Gallery in the plans for Marsh's Library, this complication threatened the progress of those genuinely interested in establishing an institution for the fine arts in Ireland.

The immediate threat was the possibility of an outcry on the publication of the Bill. The source of this possible outcry was open to speculation. It might come perhaps from members of the R.D.S., or from the supporters of Marsh's Library. Any scandal at this early stage was bound to damage the exciting new project if the controversial clauses were publicly debated, the more sensitive members of the inner circle could only hope that the idea of a National Gallery was sufficiently strong in the popular imagination that the details regarding Marsh's library would be overlooked when the time came.

Board of Trade and Navigation

More serious, however, was the long-term threat to the progress of the new building. If, as Young suggested, it was to receive government aid on the grounds that the library was to be included in the plan, the grant would have to come out of some department's funds, and that department would want to have some control over the way the money was spent. In this case the department most likely to become involved was the Board of Trade and Navigation which in recent years, was gradually taking control over all of the institutions of science and art in Great Britain and Ireland.[14]

Thomas Larcom was not unaware of the danger of involving the Board of Trade and Navigation in the affairs of the National Gallery. He wrote to Young: 'The Board of Trade must be carefully kept clear of. Many think it would be better to have no grant at all than have it through that Board.' Young warned Larcom that 'refusing to take a grant through (the Board) almost amounts to refusing government assistance altogether'. It had, of course, been the Irish Institution's intention to build the Gallery' independently of Government funds. There was no suggestion at this stage that the 'plain' structure would cost any more than the £5,000 already available but presumably the extra space required to house the Marsh's Library collection would require additional finance. This now had to be allowed for. Nevertheless Young eventually agreed to omit reference to the Board from the Bill, confident that when the time came to ask for a grant the support of the Lord Lieutenant along with that of leading Irish legal and political figures would be sufficient to persuade the Government to comply.

Introduction of the Parliamentary Bill

So that threat had been averted for the time being. By the time the clauses had been developed fully by the combination of the Pigots, the Lord Chancellor, Young and Larcom it was June 1854 and the parliamentary session was due to end in August. The general committees of the Irish Institution and of the Dargan Committee had yet to be consulted before the Bill could be printed and circulated in Westminster. On the 28th June a joint meeting of delegations from both the Dargan Committee and the Irish Institution was held. The Dargan Committee organised the meeting and only a brief excerpt of the minutes is available in the Gallery archive. It states that the meeting 'considered the wish of Sir John Young to remove Marsh's Library to the ground of the Royal Dublin Society...to be... carried out in connection with the erection of the proposed National Gallery of Ireland'. Richard Griffith and Frederick Clarendon were in attendance. The meeting resolved to accept the proposal and the resolution was sent to the federal committees of the two bodies for approval. On the 4th July 1854 the Irish Institution adopted the motion.

On the 20th July Viscount Canning introduced the National Gallery Bill in the House of Lords for its first reading. It contained fifteen clauses. A preamble, written by the Lord Chancellor, Maziere Brady, referring to the public service of William Dargan, did not arrive in London in time for the first printing. Apparently members of the Dargan Committee were not satisfied by the treatment accorded to Dargan by the Irish Institution and were voicing complaints. However, recognising that the Lord Chancellor's preamble would be incorporated in the Act in due course, Larcom was sure that 'this mention in an Act of Parliament which will continue so long as the English Language and laws endure will be a more lasting monument than any that can be raised.' The preamble was left to one side just in case there might be any further amendments to the Bill which might have to be included as it progressed through the Parliamentary process.

Amendments to the Bill

And amendments there were. On the 20th July, Larcom received a note from Lord Talbot de Malahide, who had discussed the Bill with him recently; Talbot noted that: 'the ground on which it is proposed to build the National Gallery is in the occupation of the Royal Dublin Society and although they were quite willing to give it at ... (a reasonable?) ... rent to the Irish Institution they would expect to be mentioned in the matter'. The following day Larcom received another note on the same subject, this time from Richard Griffith; 'I have just had a visit from Lord Talbot de Malahide. He is anxious that the Bill should give power to Sidney Herbert to give a sufficient lease of the lawn to the Royal Dublin Society, that the Society should take the lease, and that the National Gallery and Library should be tenants to the Society'.[15]

It would seem that it was the members of the R.D.S. rather than the supporters of Marsh's library who had been the source of potential dissatisfaction, for this was precisely the sort of reaction that the *ad hoc* committee had dreaded would occur when the details of the Bill became public. On the 26th July, John Pigot wrote of his annoyance to Larcom. He told him that he had been under the impression that the discussions which had taken place between the Society and Herbert's solicitor, Mr. Vernon, had concluded in an arrangement for two separate leases, and he was assuming that the Society would make its own plans to obtain a lease for the larger part of the lawn. He pointed out that while he did not object to the Society availing of the convenient opportunity to have a clause included empowering Herbert to grant a lease to it also, he suspected ulterior motives and was prepared to take drastic action to avoid the Society obtaining control of the Gallery. He wrote: 'If ... the Royal Dublin Society make any serious attempt to control us, or even to get so much as the shadow of a share in our concern, then certainly I should for one go to the length of preferring to give up that site altogether and' he continued 'as the Dargan Testimonial people have all along had quite an equal suspicion of the R.D.S. there would be no difficulty from them, I imagine, if at the last moment we resolved to build elsewhere, an arrangement which even as things now are has its supporters among us and among them the Lord Chancellor'.

But there was little time to sort out the problem satisfactorily. The session was due to end shortly and if the Bill were left over to the following session other interested parties, most notably Marsh's Library, would have time to organise opposition to it which could have jeopardised the entire National

Gallery project. So it was essential that some agreement be reached. Both David and John Pigot wrote anxious letters to Larcom. The former wanted to ensure that, above all, no changes should be made in clause 3 of the Bill 'Persons enabled to make leases for the purposes of this Act' for it had been written in such general terms that the trustees were not obliged to build the Gallery on Leinster Lawn.

As a result of these discussions Larcom wrote to Young on the 4th and the 6th August proposing ways in which the clauses could be amended but his letters arrived too late. The Bill had been considered at the committee level and has been read for the third time on the 5th August. The Bill as read had been altered since it arrived in London and now met with the Chief Secretary's approval.

It would seem that John Young, who was shortly to be appointed to the position of Lord High Commissioner of the Ionian Islands, had devised the amendments with the assistance of Abraham Brewster M.P. (1796-1874), a future Lord Chancellor of Ireland. In answer to Larcom's letter of the 6th August Young expressed the wish that the alterations 'would not have the evil effects you seem to dread from the jealousy and fractiousness of the parties which by the way must be excessive if they prevail to such a lamentable extent'. The compromise he had reached was that a clause permitting the R.D.S. to take a lease from Herbert for the entire lawn would be included with no reference to the Institution or the Gallery; then, when the Society had taken the Lease, the Board of Trade would divide the land and fix the rent 'according to conditions ... as [it] shall seem meet'. In addition Young included the President and senior Vice-President of the Society as *ex-officio* members of the Board of Governors and Guardians and because the Lord Lieutenant was the President of the Society, Young pointed out, 'the Vice-President is only one out of sixteen ... the fifteen ought be able to master and manage him'. He told Larcom that he had got the agreement of the Society to these amendments but he did not give his Under-Secretary, or any members of the Irish Institution, Dargan Committee, or Marsh's Library the opportunity to comment on this arrangement. Thus the Board of Trade and Navigation had entered by a different route into the plans for the National Gallery building and was now, by this amendment, inextricably involved in the project, effectively having the final word about any plans that might be made for it.

Act of Parliament

On the 10th August 1854 'An Act to establish a National Gallery of Ireland and for the care of a public library' was passed by Parliament.

As we know today, Archbishop Marsh's collection of books was never transferred to Merrion Square. In 1862 Benjamin Lee Guinness undertook the restoration of St. Patrick's Cathedral, and agreed to renovate the Library building as well. By that time, however, the abandonment of the proposal for transfer was too late to have any effect on the design of the Gallery building, and as we shall see, the space for the Library did form part of the building as designed.

With the appointment of a Board of Governors and Guardians by the Act, the Irish Institution disengaged itself from the daily activities of establishing a National Gallery. It continue to hold annual loan exhibitions until 1860 when, satisfied that its functions could be fully taken over by the Gallery Board, it disbanded. Of course the most active members of the Institution were among the Governors of the Gallery so the change of forum did not interfere with progress of the Gallery. In fact it probably assisted it by reducing the number of people attending any one meeting.

As with the Institution, most of the members of the Gallery Board concentrated on assembling a national collection of the fine arts. The Building Trustees, with the assistance of a sub-committee appointed by the Board, assumed responsibility for the building. They presented regular reports to the Board with which all final decisions rested.

CHAPTER II

Preparation 1854-1859

Request for a Grant

The design for the Natural History Museum had already been prepared when the Board of Governors and Guardians of the National Gallery met for the first time on the 13th January 1855 at the Royal Hibernian Academy headquarters in Abbey Street. Using the estimated cost of this design, Richard Griffith calculated that a building for the National Gallery and Marsh's Library would cost £11,000, £1,000 more than the Museum because of the difference in length between the two sites; they were parallel to one another but not at right angles to Leinster House, and for this reason the Gallery site was forty-two feet longer. Consequently Griffith assumed that the Gallery building would be 'considerably longer'. This discrepancy between the two supposedly symmetrical buildings was not questioned in detail until a much later stage, when it was to cause considerable financial embarrassment.

Without further investigation into costs the Board addressed a memorial to the Lord Lieutenant the Earl of St. Germans, requesting a grant of £6,000 —the difference between the Dargan Committee fund and Griffith's estimate. The Treasury, from whose class VII 'temporary and special fund', the grant would be given, contacted Griffith during the following months. Although Griffith told them that the money would not be necessary during the present year a grant of £3,000 was voted on 31st July 1855, and a grant of £3,000 was to be voted the following year.[16]

George Mulvany's design

George Mulvany, who was now the Honorary Secretary of the Board, as well as of the Irish Institution, undertook the task of preparing an internal design for the Gallery and the Library. Although he never claimed to be an architect he was a competent artist as his drawings indicate (illus. 19). His ground plan depicts a rectangular building two hundred and fifty-seven feet long, generally similar to the Natural History Museum with an out-building projecting forty feet wide by about one hundred feet long on the north elevation. His entrance in the centre of the southern elevation contravened the R.D.S. proposal on the symmetry of the wings of Leinster House because the Museum entrance was,

at the time, also in its southern elevation. For this reason it is probable that the entrance detail was very simple although we cannot be sure because Mulvany never produced any external views. However, any simplicity of elevation at the entrance was certainly balanced by the grand scale of the vestibule. In the large rectangular hallway, two stories high, the predominant feature was a series of tall stone columns, four along each side of the hall supporting a balcony at the first floor level, and two framing the main stair which lay at the opposite end of the vestibule facing the entrance door. Off the ground floor, forming wings to the central hall were the sculpture hall and library; above these, with access from the balconies were the other two major apartments, the picture galleries (illus. 20 and 21).

On the 5th November 1855 the Board 'approved generally of the plans laid on the table by Messrs Mulvany, Pigot, Stronge and Pigot' and ordered

19. *Transverse section of proposed hall and staircase by George Mulvany, signed by Robert Travers, Assistant Librarian, 2 March 1856, and by Lord Talbot de Malahide, Chairman of the Dargan Committee, 2 April 1856. N.G.I. cat. no. 18,098.*

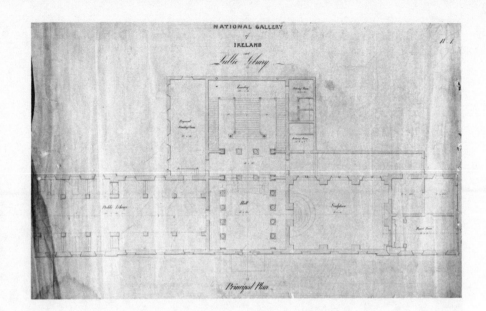

20. *Ground floor plan of proposed*
National Gallery and public
library by George Mulvany.
The pencil sketches in the hall
and sculpture hall are possibly
by or after Charles Lanyon.
N.G.I. cat. no. 18,099.

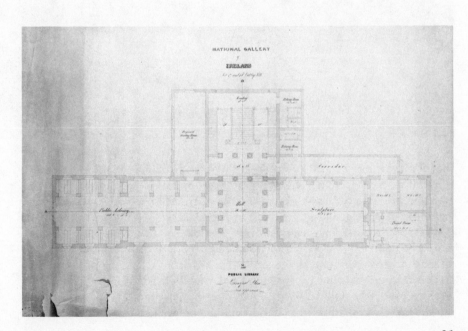

21. *First floor plan of proposed*
National Gallery and public
library by George Mulvany.
N.G.I. cat. no. 18,903.

that the drawings be sent to the Board of Marsh's Library and the Dargan Committee for approval. The drawings were initialled by Robert Travers, assistant librarian of Marsh's Library on the 24th March 1856, and signed by Lord Talbot de Malahide, Chairman of the Dargan Committee on the 2nd April 1856. It must have seemed quite possible then that the new Gallery would be completed shortly after the Museum, on which construction had already started (illus. 22). However, Richard Griffith was dubious about the structural merit of Mulvany's proposal and consulted Jacob Owen, then Chief Architect with the Board of Works. After examining them Owen wrote 'I feel myself greatly embarrassed in deciding what report I ought to make on his

22. *The Natural History Museum before 1908. The entrance door was moved to its present position on the east elevation shortly afterwards. Reproduced by kind permission of the National Museum of Ireland.*

23. *Bank of Ireland, College Green, roof of cash office designed by Francis Johnston. Published in* Bank of Ireland Bicentenary Essays; *Photograph by Pieterse Davison International.*

plans;... the rooms are well adaptable but the drawings... are so unfinished and show so manifest a want of experience in the treatment of many important practical points that I venture to hope Mr. Mulvany has already discovered the difficulties with which the task is surrounded and will be induced to abandon the office he has undertaken in so liberal a spirit'.

He went on to note some of the major deficiencies, one of which was the roof; he stated that when he had talked to Mulvany about it, the latter had 'referred to the roof of the cash office in the Bank of Ireland which I inspected with him; but this is a construction so costly and injudicious as to preclude its adoption as a precedent'. Owen also mentioned that no allowance had been made for the slope in the site, suggesting that it would be suitable to add an extensive basement area to the building. He concluded his criticisms by saying 'no prudent builder would undertake a construction on a document so defective in necessary information, or if he did it would be open door to extra claims that would be found very embarrassing' (illus. 23).

24. *Custom House, Belfast,*
designed by Charles Lanyon.
Lawrence Collection, National
Library of Ireland.

The reaction that this report was bound to cause among the founders of the National Gallery worried Griffith to the extent that he attached the following warning to it before he sent it to Larcom: 'you will not mention Owen's report to anyone but the Lord Chancellor as it would cause a blow up if made public'. He hoped to avoid any controversy by inviting a professional architect to design the roof and fill in basic details. He mentioned the names of Frederick Clarendon, who designed the Natural History Museum, and John Skipton Mulvany, George's brother, both of whom he thought, might agree to take on the job at little or, possibly, no cost. We have no record as to whether or not they were approached, nor, indeed, do we have any record of the approach which must have been made to Sir Charles Lanyon (1813-1889), the professional architect who in the event, did agree to complete the drawings (illus. 25).

Charles Lanyon's first design

Lanyon, who was married to Jacob Owen's daughter, Elizabeth, was a highly successful architect working in Belfast in partnership with William Lynn. He already had some of that city's principal buildings to his credit, the Courthouse and Jail, and the Custom House; and, with Lynn, the Queen's University. He was also employed by the Board of Works with responsibility for the construction of roads, bridges and railways in County Antrim, and it was

25. *Charles Lanyon, Illustrated London News 22.6.1889. Reproduced by kind permission of the Illustrated London News.*

probably this connection with Dublin that prompted Griffith to invite him to complete the National Gallery design[17] (illus. 24).

The first evidence of Lanyon's involvement with the National Gallery is a letter from him dated the 9th July 1856 by which time he had received tracings of Mulvany's drawings and was in a position to comment on them. He was not happy with the general plan of the building and wanted to make some radical changes: '...the more I think of it the more I am persuaded that the entrance should be at the end ... (facing) ... Merrion Square ...' He also noted that the hall and staircase were in the 'proportion of six to ten of the whole area of floors' adding 'this would have been a tremendous sacrifice of space'. He told Griffith that he was preparing two sketches, one with the entrance in the centre of the south elevation of the building as proposed by Mulvany and a new plan with the entrance at the east of the building facing Merrion Square.[18]

On the 17th July William Lynn (referred to as Lane in the Minute Book) attended a Board meeting bringing the sketches with him. Lanyon was serving on the Grand Jury in Belfast and could not come to Dublin. Unfortunately the sketches do not survive. However, while there is no further information about Lanyon's new plan other than that the entrance faced east, we do know of two major changes he proposed to make with Mulvany's plan; firstly he wanted to increase the length of the building by ten feet, thus making the southern elevation two hundred and sixty-seven feet; and secondly he suggested that the floor of the sculpture hall should be lowered, utilising the slope in the site to increase the height of the room. Griffith's comments on the sketches reveal further information 'Both have merit' he told Larcom 'but neither can be adopted without considerable modification. Both in extent of building as well as ornament. They are both far too expensive.'

The Board pondered over both plans for a month, during which two full Board meetings took place. The Building Committee appointed by the Board in 1855 also met, and it would seem that during one of these meetings Lanyon's new plan with the eastern entrance was adopted. Griffith was confident that the Board would also choose this plan and on the 4th August 1856 he told Larcom that he had written to the architect '...with definite instructions ... which I hope will produce a moderate plan entering from Merrion Square...' But then he began to doubt whether influential members of the Board would agree with him for on the 14th August he wrote a hurried note, 'I regret to find the Chancellor, (Maziere Brady) clings to the central entrance which I think very objectionable in many respects. At the last meeting [of the Building Committee] he had adopted the Merrion Square entrance, a petty feeling of jealousy is acting on others and he may have been influenced but I know him to be a fair minded man...' However, the Chancellor must eventually have been won over for at the Board meeting on the 21st August, 'after much dissension', Griffith was instructed to organise 'matured plans' based on Lanyon's alteration of Mulvany's plans with the southern entrance so that building could commence.

Lanyon's second design

During the following eighteen months we know that Lanyon worked on the National Gallery design, although there is only one drawing of his in the National Gallery collection. This depicts cross sections of the principal apartments of the building (illus. 26). There are, however, notes sent to Griffith giving sketchy outlines of the changes as they occurred. The first of these was sent from Belfast on the 2nd September 1856. Lanyon wrote 'We

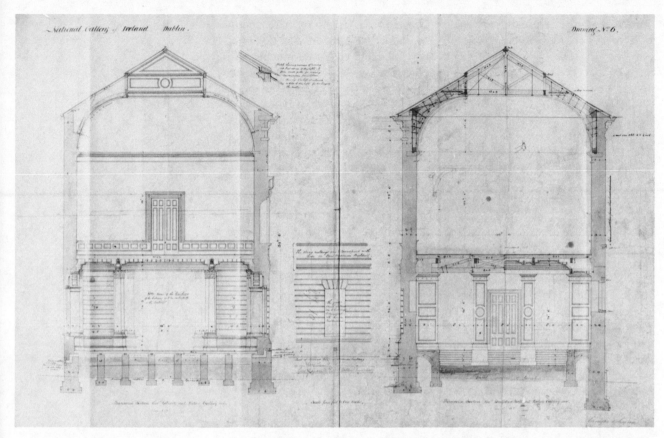

26. Transverse section through the library/picture gallery (left) and sculpture hall/picture gallery (right) of the proposed National Gallery by Charles Lanyon. Signed Lanyon and Lynn, architect, November 1856. N.G.I. cat. no. 18,097.

are very anxious to make the hall very effective but do not think it desirable to make the staircase a too important feature, thereby sacrificing the utility of the hall'. It will be remembered that his first reaction to Mulvany's drawings had been to object to the disproportionate size of the vestibule. A month later however, he wrote: 'The only alteration is that instead of cutting off the Board Room from the end of the Sculpture Gallery we have given the whole length of the wing to the purpose of the Gallery and placed the Board Room in the outbuilding having the porter's residence underneath the same for which arrangement the ground is well suited.' Lynn had commented that the presence of a residential house, adjoining the site, (now no. 86 Merrion Square) was 'an advantage in completely concealing the rear of the building' thus allowing the original staircase protrusion to be increased with no noticeable interference in the appearance of the structure in the context of Leinster Lawn.

37

While these alterations were going on, Griffith was becoming increasingly agitated about the possible cost. He was aware that Lanyon was not only increasing the size of the building but was also adding elaborate touches. He consulted Cockburn and Son, the contractors who were already working on the Natural History Museum, and together they arrived at an estimate of £27,000, a staggering increase on the budget of £11,000 already available. In October 1856 he wrote to Larcom in despair 'I have cautioned and recautioned Lanyon regarding expense on his plans, but he said to carry out the entrance from the centre and make a handsome hall and staircase suited to the entrance to a building two hundred and fifty feet long, little less that would be suitable could be done...' He concluded the letter with a suggestion which he proposed to put to the Board: '...at the present time the design to be executed should be limited to the oblong building without any projection for a staircase behind... according to this arrangement the building might be erected and a sufficient portion completed for say £12,000 or £12,800 — but, you will say, we must have a staircase and so you shall, a temporary one'.

He enclosed a pencil sketch which depicted the ground plan of the oblong building similar to Mulvany's one, with a staircase attached in the place of the intended one which, had the proportions been taken seriously, could not have been much more than a ladder.

However, despite this, Griffith's plan was well received when it was proposed at the Board meeting on the 9th February 1857, Jacob Owen and a Mr. Bell representing Lanyon being present. Lanyon's design was formally adopted, and it was agreed that construction was to take place in two stages as outlined by the Chairman of the Board of Works. With this in mind, the Building Trustees were ordered to invite tenders, to present the plans to the Council of the R.D.S., and to finalise matters relating to the occupation of the site with the Board of Trade and Navigation.*

On the 19th March the building trustees received tenders from six contractors in answer to their invitation. Cockburn and Son quoted a figure of £17,627.12.5d.; R. & J. Carolan, also of Dublin, quoted a figure which came within £54 of Cockburn's. In addition it was noted that at least £5,000 would be necessary to provide fittings for the Library and the Gallery thus bringing the overall cost to nearly £23,000. After careful examination of the tenders it emerged that the maximum saving that might be effected by leaving part of the building unfinished amounted to only £2,000. It was decided by the Trustees that the only course open to them was to extract another £12,000 from the Treasury. Any hope that Lanyon might have been able to reduce the

*On the 4th August 1855 the R.D.S. had legally acquired its portion of Leinster Lawn from Sir Sidney Herbert.

38

cost of the structure by modifying it was dashed when a letter was received from him a week later explaining why the Gallery was to cost so much more than the Natural History Museum. The principal reasons were: firstly deeper foundations were necessary because the site was on a slope, secondly, there was a difference of two hundred and fifteen thousand cubic feet in volume between the two buildings, thirdly, he planned to line the walls with hollow bricks in order to allow occupation as soon as the building was finished, and finally he proposed to spend an extra £1,000 on the internal plaster-work.

Request for an additional grant

In these circumstances a memorial was written by the Board on behalf of the Building Trustees, seeking the additional grant. This time it was addressed to the Lords of the Treasury and dated 20th April 1857. Based largely on Lanyon's letter, it included the Board's own justification of the difference in cost. The authors of the document shifted the blame from extravagant

27. *The first floor of the Natural History Museum looking east 1906. Reproduced by kind permission of the National Museum of Ireland.*

28. *The ground floor of the Natural History Museum looking West 1914. Reproduced by kind permission of the National Museum of Ireland.*

designing on the architect's part to the decision taken in 1854 committing the trustees to build on that particular site. They complained that the R.D.S. was adding unspecified expensive external decoration to the Natural History Museum which they were obliged to match, and they added that if the cutstone frontage could be dispensed with, the estimates could be significantly reduced — although hardly by £12,000. They also pointed out that the new building had to accommodate a library, a gallery and a sculpture hall whereas the museum was a single unit. After threatening to abandon the entire project they concluded the memorial with an emotive plea: 'They (the Trustees) submit that the National Gallery of Ireland has been already so recognized by the Imperial Parliament and by your Lordships as to entitle it to be considered as an object of national interest'. Details of the grants given to the National Galleries of England and Scotland were enclosed[19] (illus. 27 and 28).

The official reply from James Wilson M.P., secretary of the Treasury received some months later was a terse refusal: '…the grant of £6,000 was obtained on the distinct understanding that it should be final…' In the meantime, however, the points which the Board members had raised did not fall on deaf ears but were to emerge with answers as British officials and politicians were lobbied individually.

The Lord Lieutenant made the first approach. On the 4th May 1857 Larcom wrote to Wilson on his behalf stating the Lord Lieutenant's unequivocal support for the cause as cited in the memorial: 'His Excellency deems it only due to the great National object which it is sought by this Gallery to obtain, that he should express to the Lords Commissioners of the Treasury his warm concurrence in the prayer of the Memorial'. Wilson, unmoved, expanded little on his reply to the Board 'I am commanded … to acquaint you, for the information of his Excellency the Lord Lieutenant that the grant of £6,000 … was made on the distinct understanding that it would be final.'

On the 20th May, Edward Senior, who was a civil servant and a member of the Irish Institution, wrote to Larcom offering to discuss the Gallery's financial problem with 'a very old friend', G. Lewis who was an official in the Treasury. Larcom accepted his offer and a fortnight later he received discouraging information. Senior's report was brief and to the point. He said that Lewis' 'misimpressions were that the object was to provide a magnificent building as an ornament to Dublin at the cost of imperial funds. That a smaller and plainer building quite adequate to the wants of Dublin could be provided for £11,000. That the site might be changed. That Dublin had other libraries and that the removal (of Marsh's Library) was not necessary'. The Treasury official would seem to have taken exception to the final thrust of the Board's recent memorial.

A week later Griffith was in London and took the opportunity to speak to Wilson about the National Gallery. His report to Larcom was equally discouraging '[Wilson] says, no doubt he says truly, that a detailed plan and estimate, by a competent architect, should have been obtained before any application was made to the Treasury; in vain I explained to him that the mistake arose from a rough estimate having been made based on the proportionate lengths of the trunk of the National Gallery as compared to the trunk of the Museum for the Royal Dublin Society, but that in that very estimate the differences in the internal construction of the National Gallery and the Library were not taken into consideration nor the detail of the fitments etc. necessary to complete the building, suited to the purposes to which it was to be applied…' Wilson, clearly unimpressed with this argument had countered by mentioning that he had received an application for the Gallery Board for a large grant to buy paintings which 'no doubt would be repeated…even if the building was completed…' adding '…the Treasury cannot undertake to furnish and support *provincial galleries...*'. Before Griffith met Wilson again, four days later, he consulted Maziere Brady on this point and received a pledge from him that no further grant for paintings would be requested if the money to complete the building was sanctioned. But when Griffith conveyed this message to Wilson the latter reacted by looking '...doubtful as much as to say I do not believe you'. In June Griffith had an interview with the Prime Minister, Lord Palmerston, who responded in a 'friendly' manner, but was quite adamant that no further money was available, explaining that '...in the present temper of Parliament it is impossible to carry grants for local establishments'.

In Autumn 1857 the Irish Institution, which had had little formal contact with the National Gallery Board since August 1854, began organising a Memorial on a grand scale in support of the Gallery's quest for additional finance. The plan was to invite the illustrious list of members of the Institution to endorse the petition culminating with a deputation consisting of members of both Houses of Parliament which would deliver the Memorial to the Chancellor of the Exchequer. In November 1857 George Mulvany and J. Calvert Stronge, who were still the honorary secretaries of the Institution, sent out letters inviting members to sign and enclosing with each a copy of the petition. The initial reaction was not favourable. Mulvany's report to the Committee on the 5th January 1858 mentioned that, among others, the Earls of Eglinton, Cork and Derby had declined the invitation; the Duke of Leinster also refused to sign because in his opinion it was an inappropriate time to ask the Government for money. The Lord Lieutenant signed it provisionally but added 'I have doubts whether it conflicts with the station of Viceroy to sign an appeal to the Treasury for a grant of public money...however friendly I feel to the object...' His signature was not used.[20]

And there were objections to the design of the building, two of which came from senior vice-presidents of the R.D.S., the Earl of Clancarty and Lundy Foot. In a letter dated 29th November 1857 Clancarty wanted to know why so much money was necessary for the Gallery building: 'The sum now to be applied for, joined with what is already in hand, will be more than double the amount of what, I believe, was the cost of erecting the right wing, and I am therefore apprehensive that the design for the elevation of the Gallery, however abstractly good, may be upon a scale too large, or in a style too rich to be properly consistent with it'. On receiving an assurance from George Mulvany telling him that 'by agreement with the R.D.S. council', the wings would correspond externally, Clancarty agreed not only to sign the petition but also to join the deputation. Lundy Foot's complaint, dated the 30th November, was based on 'erroneous statements put before the public in reference...to the Royal Dublin Society'; he cited an entry in Thom's

Directory 1857, which stated that the R.D.S. and the National Gallery of Ireland had already come to an agreement, and that 'a spacious gallery is now in course of erection'. He pointed out 'that the elevation of the intended Gallery has been objected to, for want of uniformity with the society's Museum already built'. Both letters were forwarded to the National Gallery trustees.

At this stage, Griffith was already aware that the progress on the design was being observed with disapproval by the R.D.S., and on the 5th December 1857 he felt it necessary to draw the Board's attention to the fact that 'several influential members' of the Society had voiced 'strong objections' to Lanyon's design adding that if full approval was not forthcoming from the Society's council there was little hope that the Department of Science and Art would agree to finalise the land agreement. This latest problem, coupled with the ongoing financial one, forced the Board to drop Lanyon's design until the trustees could extract a more modest one from him.

Sanction of an additional grant

Shrugging off these difficulties, the Irish Institution persevered with its memorial. Then in February 1858 the outlook changed dramatically. Palmerston's government was defeated on a vote in the House of Commons, and was replaced by an unstable Conservative Government led by Lord Derby. Therefore when the Institution's deputation, which included twenty-six Irish M.P.'s waited on the Chancellor of the Exchequer on the 24th June 1858 it was Benjamin Disraeli who received them. Lord Talbot de Malahide introduced the deputation and read the address which outlined the turbulent history of the National Gallery building project to date. Disraeli, obviously impressed not only by the eloquent speech but also, no doubt, by the presence of twenty-six valuable parliamentary votes, replied: 'Gentlemen, it affords me very great pleasure to receive a deputation from Ireland on a subject so agreeable to one's feelings at the present. There has been a great and very gratifying change in the nature of the Irish deputations of late years. You used to come to complain of troubles in your country, but now you have happily become more prosperous. Next you came on the subject of the promotion of your national industry, to which you were then devoting considerable attention; and now you have advanced another point, and have directed your attention to the promotion of the fine arts. I shall be very happy to do what I can to advance your object. ...On the understanding that the sum required this year will not exceed £5,000, and subject to a conversation with Sir Richard Griffith as to the details, I shall be disposed to recommend the Government to accede to your request. In my opinion this is one of those objects which it is the duty of the

29. *Lord Derby, Prime Minister 1858, by Samuel Lawrence. Reproduced by kind permission of the Trustees of the National Portrait Gallery, London.*

Government to support, and as I have been obliged to call upon Ireland to assist me in putting the finances of the country in order, I feel disposed to do what I can to serve you in return'. So at last, there was to be enough money to construct the building as designed by Lanyon[21] (illus. 29 and 30).

Lanyon's final design

Unknown however, to most of the people involved in the project and perhaps to Disraeli as well, further problems had already arisen. Firstly Lanyon had again modified his own south entrance design which had been abandoned by

44

30. Benjamin Disraeli, first Lord Beaconsfield, Chancellor of the Exchequer 1858 by John Everett Millais. Reproduced by kind permission of the Trustees of the National Portrait Gallery, London.

the Board in December 1857 and had produced two revised proposals, one of which again brought the entrance door from the southern elevation to the eastern end of the building. The only available evidence of this revised design is a ground plan of Leinster Lawn with the area of his proposed building shaded in (illus. 34). This indicates that the size of the outbuilding on the northern elevation had been increased to such an extent as to double the original width of the eastern elevation. John Pigot is on record as stating that Lanyon's final design was 'Deficient and objectionable both in point of taste and convenience… interior totally wanting in — unity…entrance externally mean and internally inconvenient and unsightly…' There is no evidence of a formal request to Lanyon to prepare such a design.

45

Francis Fowke

Secondly in May 1858 Sir Henry Cole, Secretary to the Department of Science and Art, which had taken over all responsibility for cultural institutions from the Board of Trade and Navigation in 1857, and which therefore now had to approve the design before construction could actually start, had intervened by dispatching to Dublin one of his inspectors, Francis Fowke, to ascertain the cause of the delay with the whole project (illus. 31). Fowke's visit was to change the whole concept of the building (illus. 32).

32. *Captain Francis Fowke R.E.
(1823-1865). Illustrated
London News, 3.5.1862.
Reproduced by kind permission
of the Illustrated London News.*

Francis Fowke (1823-1865) a captain of the Royal Engineers and an inspector with the Department of Science and Art was ideally suited to sorting out the problems faced by the Building Trustees, having recently designed a gallery in the South Kensington Museum (now the Victoria and Albert Museum) for the Sheepshanks Gift. In this he was associated with Richard Redgrave who had discovered a formula for the horizontal, non-glare lighting of picture galleries; Fowke went on to develop an arrangement for lighting with gas. In addition he gained experience with the use of a new form of patented fire-proof flooring which he erected in the South Kensington Museum. During his brief career Fowke was involved in numerous and

33. *The Sheepshanks Gallery in the South Kensington Museum (The Victoria and Albert Museum); it was designed in 1856 by Francis Fowke with gas lighting, and constructed according to the Fox and Barrett fire-proof floor patent. Reproduced by kind permission of the Victoria and Albert Museum.*

diverse activities for both the army and the Department of Science and Art, acquiring a reputation for the ability to carry out jobs at low cost[22] (illus. 33).

Ostensibly Fowke's purpose in coming to Dublin was to report on the state of the project and the reasons for the delay. After all, from Cole's point of view, there was no apparent cause for the delay — the site was available, the building was supposed to be similar to one already completed and the money as originally requested by the Building Trustees was also available. With a budget of one million pounds for the promotion of science and art throughout Great Britain and Ireland, and a number of large and important projects underway on the mainland, it was in Cole's interest to keep the cost of the Dublin project as low as possible, even though the monies were not coming directly out of his department's funds. Griffith was slightly suspicious of Fowke's function in Ireland. He confided to Larcom 'I had a long conversation and discussion yesterday with Captain Fowke and I find *(entre nous)* that *in his instructions* he was directed to prepare a design for the Gallery which if possible, could be erected for about £11,000'. Nevertheless he was optimistic about the outcome of the Irish Institution's deputation and decided to facilitate Fowke who, he said, was 'very clear in details' and might be able to make some useful comments.

However, following the success of the deputation in June 1858 the real reason for Fowke's visit became apparent. When Griffith sent a request to Henry Cole asking him to arrange the tenure of the site as laid down by the

National Gallery Act of 1854, he received the following reply in a letter dated 26 July 1858 'Referring to your letter of the 26th ult., enclosing copies of the transactions which have taken place between the Governors of the National Gallery of Dublin, the Building Trustees and the Royal Dublin Society, on the subject of Leinster Lawn, I am directed by the Lords of the Committee of Council on Education to inform you that the correspondence has been passed to Captain Fowke, R.E., who has been requested to report on the plans which it is proposed to adopt, before the Board enters into the consideration of the question of ground rent'. Griffith was annoyed; he wrote to Larcom: 'I fear this busybody Mr. Cole will trouble us…It appears to me that under the advice of Mr. Cole Lord Salisbury's committee are arrogating to themselves more power than they are invested with by the Act…', but, he added, 'no change can be admitted in regard to the length of the building…' It transpired nevertheless that Salisbury's committee — the Committee of the Council on Education, which held the Department of Science and Art under its jurisdiction — had indeed been given a legal right of veto as a result of John Young's haste in introducing the 1854 National Gallery Bill in Parliament. Clause 17 of the Act stated: '…it shall be lawful for such Society (R.D.S.) to divide the Lands and Premises which shall be comprised therein in such Proportions, and under such Conditions and Restrictions, as to the Board of Trade and Navigation shall seem meet…' Cole was obviously not going to allow the Irish Gallery have any more Government money than was absolutely necessary despite an unstable government. The only suggestions Griffith could make to counteract this power were either to buy the land outright or to ask G.A. Hamilton, an Irish M.P., who had promoted the Gallery in Parliament consistently, if he could do anything to make Cole 'work'. Nothing came of either of these suggestions.

The Department remained silent for a month after this devastating communication while Griffith became increasingly anxious; he wanted to lay the foundations before the onset of winter and was getting to the stage when he would have gone ahead without permission. Then, at the end of August, Fowke wrote to him from Paris where he was working on the River Danube Navigation Commission. He enclosed a small copy of his proposed modification of Lanyon's design which he had prepared as a result of his visit to Dublin. In a letter to Larcom, Griffith admitted that he did not fully understand the plan but thought that it might be suitable. On the 6th September he received a note from an official in the Department of Science and Art which stated that the sanction to proceed would be given shortly. Finally on the 23rd September Griffith received a lengthy report, containing an outline of Fowke's proposals for the National Gallery building which he had already presented to Lord Salisbury and for which he had received approval.[23] The report included details of dimensions and costs of Fowke's 'modification of the original design' as well as arguments explaining why his plan was better than any of the previous plans submitted to the building trustees. This latest design bore little relation to either Mulvany's or Lanyon's efforts. Fowke had copied the external dimensions of the Natural History Museum exactly, and prepared his own internal arrangement. He put the total estimated cost of his plan at £17,000, £6,000 more than the Gallery's original budget but also a saving of £6,000 on the Gallery's final budget.

Approval of Fowke's design

There was little Griffith could do now and, although there is no evidence of his reaction to the merits of the report, it would seem that he was not too displeased with the design. The Lord Chancellor and George Mulvany had already informed Griffith of their satisfaction with the new plan, Mulvany noting that he thought it was somewhat similar to his own design. On the 1st October 1858 Griffith read the report to the Board of Governors and Guardians. It then went through the procedure of being approved by the other institutions — the Royal Dublin Society, the Dargan Committee and Marsh's Library. There must have been a certain lack of interest now for no objections were raised. Larcom wrote to Lanyon explaining the difficulties with the Board of Trade, enclosing a cheque for £600 of work done. Griffith approached the Department of Science and Art for the last time with all of the necessary documents to obtain the official approval; after hesitating briefly, Salisbury's committee put a rent of £100 in perpetuity on the Leinster Lawn site at a meeting on the 9th November. The speech to be read by the Lord Lieutenant at the ceremony of the laying of the first stone could be written at last.

CHAPTER III

Construction 1859-1864

External symmetry

In make to make the National Gallery building a mirror image of the Natural History Museum, Fowke had to deal with the asymmetry of Leinster Lawn. Of Lanyon's solution to the problem he was scathing: 'In the former design the uniformity of the minor parts (i.e., the screen wall behind and the Lawn in front of the Gallery) is obtained at the expense of the most prominent object, the buildings, a proceeding which must surely be erroneous in principle besides being costly in execution'. So his proposal was to keep the buildings of equal dimension and to lengthen the minor parts, the lawn by sixteen feet and the wall by twenty-four feet, in such a way that the difference would be barely perceptible[24] (illus. 34).

It was principally in the design of the interior that Fowke had the opportunity to display his architectural ability. It was necessary that he prove himself in the eyes of the Building Trustees since he had, after all, been imposed upon them by civil servant to replace a well-established and admired Irish architect. Fowke's approach to the design was to create the most functional building possible within the financial and spatial limits dictated by the choice of site.

Ground plan

The ground plan of the original Gallery has not changed significantly over the years; the eastward slope in the site provided room for a basement as Jacob Owen had suggested; and this was now used for a dwelling for a resident attendant, as well as for extensive storage space. Above this what is now the large paintings room (No. 1a) on the ground floor was the Sculpture Hall; the present Italian room (No. 9) was for paintings, and the smaller rooms (Nos. 10-13) were for cabinet pictures, drawings, watercolours and engravings; what is today the fresco room (No. 18) was originally intended to be the Library; and the mezzanine floor (No. 14) was originally divided into smaller units containing offices and extra library space (illus 35).

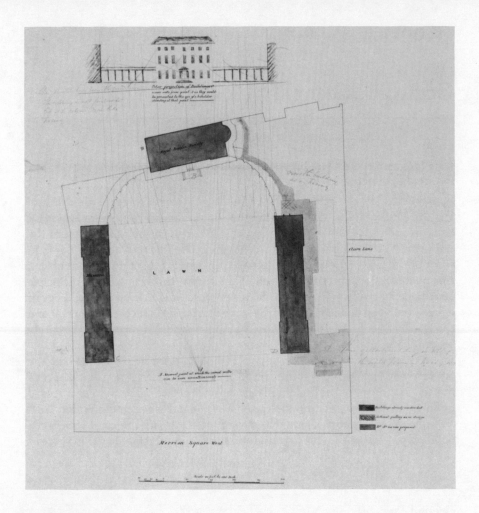

34. Polar projection of the Leinster Lawn complex by Francis Fowke, indicating the only point (a) at which the inequality in the screen walls can be observed. N.G.I. cat. no. 6890.

Sculpture Hall

Fowke's modification of Lanyon's Sculpture Hall consisted primarily of raising the floor at the east end of the building to ground level. Lanyon had proposed having this floor about five feet lower so that one would have descended a short flight of steps on entering the room. In order to increase the 'apparent height of the room' which he found wanting as a result of raising the floor, Fowke replaced the pilasters of Lanyon's design with Corinthian columns. These columns in turn carried an entablature concealing the ventilation system. This alteration to the floor level made it possible to have a significant basement area. Lanyon had probably felt that the sacrifice in the dimensions of

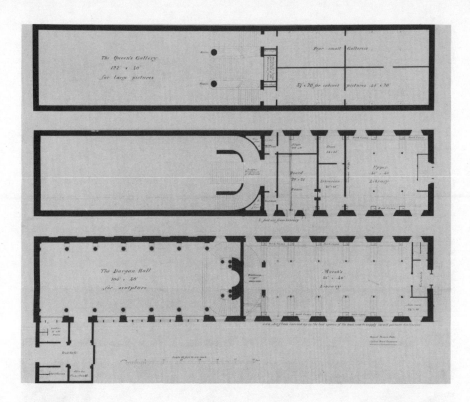

35. *Floor plan of the National
Gallery by Francis Fowke.
N.G.I. cat. no. 6917.*

the Hall was not worth such a provision. Another change Fowke made to the
Sculpture Hall was to put an alcove in the north east corner. It is hard to see the
merit of this aspect of the design for while it might have made an interesting
corner in the Hall for some special display it certainly decreased the dimensions
of the vestibule which, as we shall see, were of meagre proportions already.
This alcove was closed off when the building was extended in 1903. With large
windows on the northern wall, and two slightly smaller ones on the southern
wall the Hall was adequately lit for the exhibition of Sculpture (illus. 36).

The 'Queen's Gallery'

The main picture gallery, called the 'Queen's Gallery' was situated directly
above the Sculpture Hall. Its vast wall space was not interrupted by windows,
Fowke choosing to illuminate it entirely with 'horizontal light' i.e., a glass roof.
In a design similar to that in the Natural History Museum, it was so successful
that natural light is still used in this gallery during the day (illus. 37).

36. *Sculpture Hall, with gas lamps*
   suspended from the ceiling
   c.1900 (now room 1a),
   Lawrence Collection, National
   Library of Ireland.

37. *The Queen's Gallery (now*
   room 9).

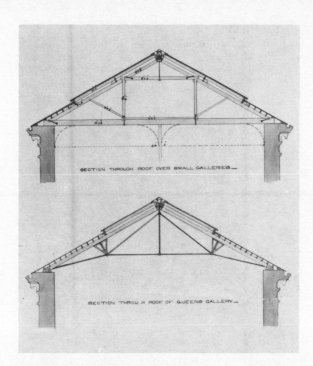

38. Section through the roof over the small galleries (above) and through the roof of the Queen's Gallery by Francis Fowke. N.G.I., cat. no. 18,046.

The four small picture galleries

Two short flights of stairs at the western end of the main picture gallery led to four small galleries for cabinet pictures located towards the west end of the building. The introduction of galleries for cabinet pictures was an essential part of Fowke's concept. He stated in his report that as 'cabinet pictures form the greater part of all British collections it becomes an important point in the construction of any gallery in this country that apartments of suitable dimensions should be provided for the exhibition of this class of pictures.' He noted that 'It is stated to be a serious defect in the far famed Dresden Gallery, that many of the small pictures of the collection are entirely lost by being hung along with the larger works...' To get these small galleries, he first raised the height of the floor to Lanyon's western first floor gallery because as the rooms were also lit from above 'the pictures should be approached as near as possible to the light'. Fowke then divided the floor into quarters with light screen walls whose weight was supported only the floor itself. He had to add extra glazed areas into the roof of this section as a result, so that each compartment would be adequately lit. The extra glazed areas were set flush with the slate roof so that the profile of the roof would not be noticeably different to that of the Museum (illus. 38).

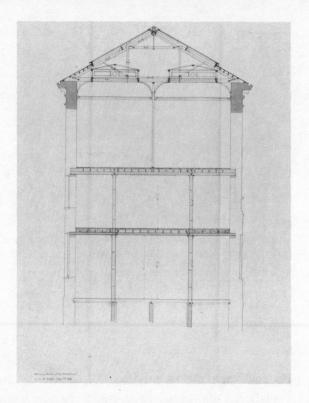

39. Traverse section through the Library on the ground floor and the mezzanine floor, and through the small picture galleries on the top floor by Francis Fowke. N.G.I., cat. no. 6958.

The Mezzanine floor

Having raised the floor of the western first floor gallery Fowke was left with either a very high ground floor apartment beneath or the option of inserting a mezzanine floor. He chose the latter course so making three floors in the space of Lanyon's two at the west end of the building. This, as he did not hesitate to emphasise to the Board, led to his being able to provide more floor space than in any of Lanyon's longer buildings. Being low, and difficult to light, the mezzanine floor was best suited to offices and other administrative areas. In order to maintain the symmetry of the buildings he could not put any large windows in the southern wall. The Board Room, with a small anteroom and a washroom, the librarian's office, and extra shelving space for Marsh's Library were all located here, each room was lit by a large window on the northern side, with a dark broom cupboard on the southern side of the floor and a tiny discreet window which Fowke insisted did not interfere with the symmetry. The walls dividing the offices were constructed with a material similar to that used on the floor above, and were thus easily removed when Deane chose to open up this floor in 1903 (illus 39).

40. *The west elevation with the proposed door to the Library and the window part of which provided light on the mezzanine floor. N.G.I., cat. no. 6930.*

41. *The west elevation today.*

Marsh's Library

The main section of Marsh's Library was to be situated on the ground floor beneath the mezzanine floor. Although it was purpose built it is unlikely that there would have been sufficient space to shelve the entire collection of books, a factor later used as an excuse not to transfer the Library. Had the Library been transferred it would have been self-contained as arranged in the original discussions, the entrance door being similar to that of the Gallery, with an avenue leading to Clare Street. There was to be a small porch and a cloakroom just inside the door. A narrow flight of stairs was designed for the south west corner connecting the main Library with the subsidary section and the offices above.[25] The National Gallery Board room was to be the only zone of communication between the two parts of the building, the door now connecting rooms la and lb of the Gallery not being inserted until a much later date. The basic structure of the Library was built during this period but because a decision not to transfer the Library was taken in 1862, the areas intended for it remained unfinished until 1881 when the Board of Governors and Guardians opened up the apartments as an extension of the Gallery (illus 40 and 41).

The Stairway

Fowke's principal 'modification' to Lanyon's design and one which changed the entire internal appearance of the building, was the 'elimination' of Lanyon's central feature, the grand hall and stairway. He decided that the stairway would be more effective and would take up less room, as well as being cheaper, if it were placed in the galleries themselves. He had to present numerous arguments to support the change for this was really the only part of the new plan which the Board forcefully contested. Of Lanyon's arrangement, Fowke suggested that 'the visitor would experience a feeling of disappointment … on finding that only two-thirds of the available space was allotted to the exhibition of works of art (but?) an entire one-third was devoted to the reception of the stair leading from one gallery to the other', exclaiming 'this is the actual proportion in the last design submitted to the committee'. To promote his design he argued that on both aesthetic and functional grounds it was superior to Lanyon's. The stairs, he pointed out, would form the 'culminating point in the scale or ornament' in the sculpture hall; the landing where the lower flights met was convenient for the mezzanine floor, and by entering the upper gallery directly from the stairs 'the visitor would be greatly struck by its noble proportions'. In comparison he quoted the *'Sala a Croce Greca'* in the Vatican as a Gallery where this arrangement had been successful (illus. 42 and 43).

42. *Entrance to the mezzanine floor.*

43. *Raised niche and stairs in the Sculpture Hall; the door connecting the hall to room 1B (built as the library) was inserted later.*

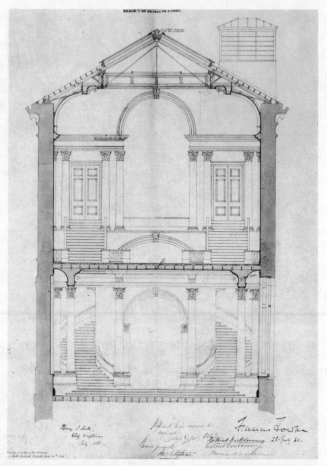

44. *Transverse section of the*
Sculpture Hall and Queen's
Gallery showing the stairway
with the raised niche on the
ground floor, and the recess
between the upper stairs.
N.G.I., cat. no. 6950.

Fowke had other uses for the stairway, one of these was to honour the chief benefactors. He intended the raised niche between the stairs to be used for the bust of Dargan, on the assumption that the hall would become popularly known as the 'Dargan Hall'. He also proposed that in the recess formed by the lateral flights of stairs leading to the four small picture galleries a fresco of Queen Victoria should be painted, this time on the assumption that the large picture gallery would be called 'the Queen's Gallery'. The Queen's fresco in turn had an additional more prosaic purpose, it functioned as the centre of the ground floor ventilation system. The foul air collected behind the elaborate frieze in the Sculpture Hall and above the bookcases in the Library, was transported through the space made by the curve in the staircase up to the open area above the recess (illus. 44).

45. Plan and sections of the vestibule roof showing the hipped roofs over the short entrance corridor, the corridor leading to the sculpture hall, and the lean-to roof over the porch at the rear. N.G.I. cat. no. 18,059.

The vestibule

Fowke's revised vestibule was perhaps his least successful 'modification'. Built as an annexe to the main building, its east elevation was merely twenty-five feet high, and sixty-five feet long. Thirty feet of this elevation was a screen wall containing, to balance the main entrance door, a kind of arch in which there was inserted a small and mean doorway which led to nothing more than a back yard. The surround of the entrance door is the only part of the annexe that has not been altered and this can still be seen within the portico built during the 1903 extension. In the original vestibule there was a short corridor, directly inside the entrance door, with a porter's room and a W.C. on the right. There was another corridor at right angles to this, with the entrance to the Sculpture Hall at one end, and a window at the other. At the rear, through a set of swing doors, was another W.C. and a small porch with a door opening into the back yard. Fowke's vestibule, therefore, was functional, adding little to the attractiveness of the building — it is hardly surprising that it was the one area of the original structure to be radically altered during both of the later extensions, in 1903 and 1968 (illus. 45, 46 and 47).

Gas lighting

Looking back at the project from this distance in time, it may be that Fowke's most significant contribution to the work will be seen in his introduction of

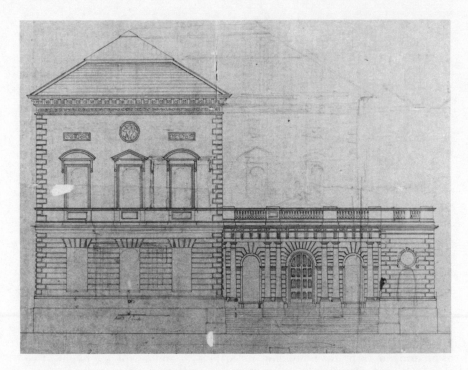

46. Proposed design of the east elevation, showing columns and a balustrade. This proposal was not adopted. N.G.I. cat. no. 6899.

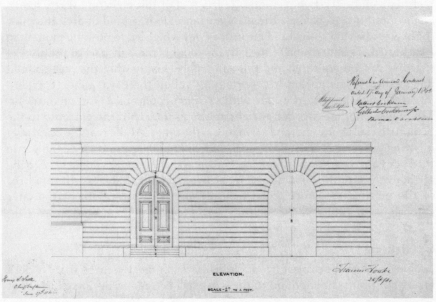

47. Final design for the east elevation by Francis Fowke. N.G.I., cat. no. 6978.

ELEVATION.

SCALE ¼" TO A FOOT.

elements in construction and lighting which were extremely novel and advanced at the time. Fowke's involvement with the South Kensington Museum had brought him directly into contact with the most recent developments in museum and gallery environment, and he clearly used his knowledge to advantage in the Dublin project.

Fowke was a member of a five man Commission appointed 'to consider the subject of lighting picture galleries by gas'. The Commission carried out extensive experiments over a period of two years in which apartments with and without gas lighting were monitored and the works of art carefully noted for any reaction. The results gave no indication of a damaging reaction to paintings from gas but some of the objects under surveillance did show signs of chemical change. However, the Commission decided that this reaction was 'due to either a town atmosphere or want of ventilation'. The report concluded that 'there is nothing innate in coal gas which renders its application to the illumination of picture galleries objectionable. Its light, though not so white as that of the sun, is equally harmless; its radiant heat may be rendered by placing a sufficient distance between the gas jets and the pictures, while the heat of combustion may be rendered eminently serviceable in promoting ventilation'.

The Irish Institution and the Board of Governors and Guardians of the Gallery had discussed this matter frequently, and even though the Institution used gas lighting for evening showings of its annual exhibitions, neither group was ever quite satisfied that it was a completely safe method. Nevertheless, Fowke was confident that its installation would be to the benefit of the Gallery. Thus the Sculpture Hall was illuminated by six gas-burners of sixty lights each, and the great picture room contained the extraordinary number of two thousand gas jets suspended from a massive oblong frame. The Hibernian Gas Company, under the superintendence of Mr. Claffey, was responsible for its assembly. No provision was yet made for lighting the Library.

Floor construction

Another significant innovation made by Fowke in the building was the method he used to construct the suspended floors. As was customary at the time, Lanyon had intended to construct the floors with timber. However, Fowke used the patented Fox and Barrett fire-proof floor system. Basically this consisted of wrought iron joists resting on girders of the same material, and partially encased in concrete which also formed the structural floor surface. It was, in fact, a forerunner of the modern method of reinforced concrete, and it is possible that this was the first time it was used in Ireland. It had originally been designed in the 1840's by Charles Fox and Henry Barrett for use in

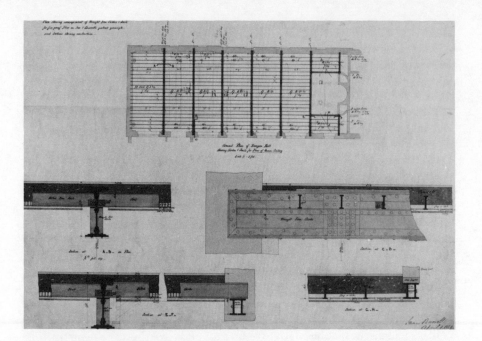

48. *Details of Iron work for floor of Queen's Gallery based on patent designed by Charles Fox and Henry Barrett, signed by James Barrett. N.G.I., cat. no. 18,009.*

lunatic asylums in England, and was being successfully employed also in the South Kensington Museum in 1858[26] (illus. 48).

Ornamentation

The solid concrete floors influenced the ornamental aspect of the rooms. The decorative ceiling of the Sculpture Hall with its six large panels and corresponding number of smaller ones on either side concealed the deep beams used in the structure of the first floor. It allowed Fowke freedom to design elaborate patterns for the plaster work as a contrast to the austere exterior. For floor covering he used tiles made by Minton Hollins and Co., of London. He had been impressed by the effect achieved by the use of such tiles in the South Kensington Museum, the floors being, as he informed the Board, 'easily cleaned, free from dust, making but little noise when walked on, transmitting absolutely no sound to the room below, and being perfectly rigid and stiff'. The tiles were set in cement, and needed to be cleaned frequently at first to remove 'a sort of scum arising from the cement'. Fowke chose a 'quiet and harmonious' design in order to give 'such a rich carpeted look to the Gallery that the floor itself like a good carpet in a room contributes largely to the decoration of the

64

apartment.' The entire building including the Library, was laid with these tiles, but only in the upper galleries and the mezzanine floor do they now remain visible.

Construction

On the 7th January 1859 the Building Trustees entered into a contract with Messrs. Cockburn & Son, of New Brunswick Street, Dublin, for the 'execution of the excavation, draining and entire mason work of the exterior of the Gallery in conformity with the schedule of the prices appended to the tender of Messrs. Cockburn and Son which was accepted by the Building Trustees on the 6th March 1857', some two years previously. They were to be paid 90% of the stated price according as each part was completed the other 10% to be paid on completion as security for the 'performance of the contract according to the plans and specification provided'. A Committee from the Board was appointed to inspect the works from time to time. But the ultimate responsibility lay with the Building Trustees who had control of the finance, and although the Board of Works was not directly involved Richard Griffith supervised all of the work closely including, it would seem, staff members of the Board working on the Gallery site.

The Lord Lieutenant, The Earl of Eglinton, laid the first stone of the National Gallery at a ceremony on the 29th January, 1859 in the presence of a distinguished assembly, with the Band of the First Royal Dragoons playing in the background. George Mulvany read an address outlining the history of the Gallery and including reference to the difficulties the Trustees had experienced in acquiring an adequate grant from the Government. The Lord Lieutenant recognized the problems in his reply but added 'I am glad to be informed that the funds now collected are sufficient to justify you in commencing operations although this may not be adequate to all requirements which a scheme of such magnitude necessarily involves'. The struggle for adequate financing was obviously not yet over but now that the building was under way, nothing was going to stop its completion, nor indeed to interfere with the project as a whole.

Griffith was in constant contact with Fowke, who had returned to London, during the construction. Tracings, with comments attached, were sent from one to the other although few adjustments were made to the measurements as originally devised by Fowke. The building proceeded rapidly at first. Cockburn & Son seemed to experience no difficulty with the unusual floor construction, and by March 1860 the walls were finished. Cockburn & Son were awarded the contract for the roof, and the Building Trustees expressed the hope that the building would be ready for occupation early in 1861.

But although the contractors had done a similar job on the roof of the Museum problems, unfortunately not recorded, arose and it was not until October 1862 that the Board of Governors and Guardians were able to hold meetings in its permanent home. During this period the Board had not been idle. It had been getting its administration under control and assembling a collection worthy to be viewed on the Gallery's inauguration day, whenever that would be. In September 1862, George Mulvany had been appointed as the first director of the Gallery, and was responsible only to the Board. The Treasury agreed to pay him a salary of £300, out of which he appointed a registrar, Henry Killingly, giving him a salary of £70. Henry Killingly had been a clerk with the Great Exhibition committee in 1853, and was later employed by the Irish Institution. The offices which had been intended for the staff of Marsh's Library were now occupied by staff members of the National Gallery for whom no provision had previously been made. A large number of works of art had been assembled over the years since the Gallery's foundation, and had been stored in the R.H.A. premises in Abbey Street. The collection included one hundred and twelve pictures, some of which had been purchased by the Board, others which had been presented, and a small number which were on indefinite loan from the National Gallery, London. It also included one hundred watercolours bequeathed by the late Captain Taylor, and a selection of plaster casts of the Elgin Marbles in the British Museum. The Board had succeeded in extracting a grant of £2,000 from the Treasury to purchase pictures and were now seeking an annual grant. George Mulvany undertook the task of preparing a catalogue, with a biographical note on each artist, and saw it emerge from the press with just three days to spare before the formal inauguration.

Furnishing

The Gallery was furnished lavishly, the tiles providing the basic colour scheme. Massive crimson coloured blinds were placed over the windows in the Sculpture Hall which, when closed during the evening viewing would have given a warm glowing effect; the walls were painted silver grey. The walls of the picture gallery above, a much brighter room, were painted in a shade of maroon, and large ottomans upholstered in velvet of a deeper shade of the same colour were placed at intervals along the gallery. Heavy curtains of the same fabric were suspended on large ornamental brass poles, and placed at the top of the lateral flights of stairs separating the four small picture galleries from the larger ones. A large heavy oak bench was put in the centre of each of

66

49. Statue of William Dargan by Thomas Farrell, presented by the Dargan Committee to the National Gallery. N.G.I. cat. no. 8277.

the small rooms. Downstairs, the Board room was dominated by a circular table of solid oak surrounded by oak chairs, once again upholstered in crimson velvet. The Library, of course, was left unfurnished. Messrs. J. J. Byrne & Son of Henry Street provided all the furnishings.

Completion

In December 1863 Cockburn & Son put the final touch to the building by hoisting the high bronze statue of William Dargan on to its pedestal in front of the Gallery. Executed by Thomas Farrell R.H.A. it indicates most clearly the connection between Dargan and the National Gallery, and certainly underlines his association with the project most effectively (illus. 49).

At this stage the building had cost over £27,000; a further £2,000 was granted by the Treasury for internal fittings during the following two years. The contractors received almost £20,000, and Henry Barrett received £2,500 for the cast iron used in the floor construction. Although Fowke designed everything except the floor construction, including such incidentals as the railings and the decoration within the building he did not receive any fee from the Building Trustees. It is difficult to pinpoint the reason for the excessive cost of the structure, but as early as March 1859 the *Dublin Builder and Engineer* had forecast that it would indeed cost more than had been allowed in the estimate. Fortunately, however, the Trustees seemed to experience no difficulty in getting the additional grants necessary from the Treasury. Thus the Gallery cost nearly £30,000, £7,000 more than the estimate of Lanyon's first design.

References to the building during Board meetings between 1859 and 1864 are slight. There were problems with the heating system in the Queen's Gallery prior to the formal opening which probably explains the time lapse between the first Board meeting in the Gallery and the inauguration. Following the inauguration the gas system in the Sculpture Hall had to be replaced which delayed opening the Gallery to the public for some months. The Governors and Guardians also spent some time discussing dedications to famous artists both inside and outside the Gallery. Suggestions included carving inscriptions to artists onto panels and fixing them to the building, and placing busts or ornamental heads in niches inside and outside the building. Both of these suggestions were eventually dropped.

Conclusion

On the 30th January 1864, the National Gallery was formally opened by the Lord Lieutenant, the Earl of Carlisle at a glittering ceremony. It was preceeded by the unveiling of the statue of Dargan with speeches read by the Lord Lieutenant, and by Lord Talbot de Malahide and Joseph Boyce, both leading members of the Dargan Committee. Then, led by the Lord Lieutenant, the invited assembly entered the National Gallery where they were greeted by George Mulvany, flanked by others closely involved in the project. The inauguration ceremony took place in the large upper gallery where a dais had been erected at the east end. Mulvany read an address in which he did not fail to mention the ongoing struggle for an annual picture fund. The Lord Lieutenant congratulated the members of the Irish Institution, the Dargan Committee and the Board of Governors and Guardians on their enterprise despite the fact that 'the previous course of Irish History had scarcely run smooth enough to foster the growth of galleries or museums of the fine arts,

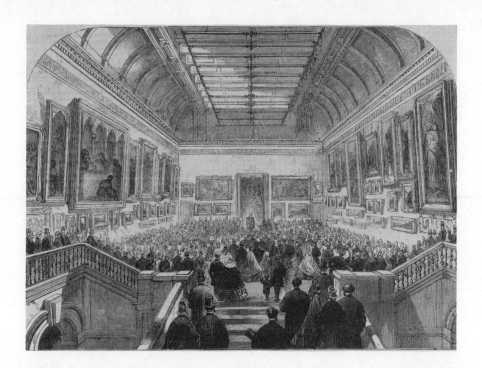

50. *The Earl of Carlisle opening the National Gallery of Ireland, 30th January 1884. Illustrated London News. Reproduced by kind permission of the Illustrated London News.*

while at the same time neither the Irish mind nor the Irish hand has shown any want of susceptibility or adaptation to them' (illus. 50).

The press reaction to the new building was generally very good, although during construction the exterior had been the subject of some harsh words. An article in *The Warder* in July 1856 had warned the public about the plan for the Lawn, the walls of the Natural History Museum having lately made their appearance: 'this moping, staring, cold strip of granite is the museum of the Dublin Society...this dreadful deposit — this opprobrium of the city — this secretion of the combined imaginations of Griffith and Hornsby... the genius of these eminent vandals'.[27] In January 1861 the Irish Times used similar terms to discuss the National Gallery: 'what noble opportunities were thrown away when the Barrack style was adopted... for the Museum and National Gallery of Leinster Lawn. These were official vandalisms, certainly, perpetrated by those whose notion of architecture for a great capital seems to consist in piling together as much stone and mortar as can be got for a given sum of money'. But in 1864 when the building was completed the criticism of the exterior was somewhat more muted; the Post noted: 'a plain structure, firmly built'; the comment of the Express: 'the exterior of the building especially under notice is neither attractive nor striking, but it presents a massive and permanent appearance'. Even the Irish Times had mellowed: 'There is nothing particularly attractive as regards the exterior except the massiveness of its style'. However the interior received almost universal approval, the Irish Times lavishing the most praise. Of the Sculpture Hall it stated: 'elegantly arranged, beautifully proportioned, and admirably adapted to its purpose', and of the picture gallery: 'we have been in many galleries, but we know of none that presents such a pleasing *coup d'oeil* in entering'. The Express was eloquent in its descriptions: 'on entering (the Sculpture Hall) you are stuck with the airy lightness and beauty of the room itself. A strange sense of richness, luxuriance and harmony creeps stealthily over you as you cast your eyes upwards and view the elegance of the decorations on the ceiling'. About the picture gallery it said 'it is noble, princely in its dimensions and its decorations are gorgeous'. The furnishings, the lighting and heating arrangements, and the colour schemes of the tiles and walls were scrutinised and lauded. The works of art were, to a large extent, ignored, although most of the newspapers wrote lengthy articles during the ensuring weeks, to make good that omission.

If then one can judge popularity by the words of the press, Francis Fowke's building was a success, and he could feel that he had anticipated the reaction of the 'visitor' with remarkable accuracy. There was only one dissenting voice, and this emanated from the Royal Institution of Architects of Ireland of which Lanyon was the Chairman. At this meeting on the 18th February 1864 a paper on the new building by W: G. Murray was read in his absence by Mr. Drew and the report on it referred to the 'meanness of the entrance and vestibule... the evident attempts to produce a striking effect in the Sculpture Hall, the general effect of which, however, is most unsatisfactory... intensely ugly, awkward and dangerous grand staircase... (and the picture gallery)... shows the same want of experience in designing... a National Gallery from which architecture is excluded...' It was ordered that the paper should be published. At the R.I.A.I. meeting of the following November the reaction of the public to the paper was recorded: '...it must be confessed without producing much effect, which is principally to be attributed to the fact that the Dublin public have not yet received sufficient education in art to appreciate good architecture or to recognise either its presence or absence in a building'.

In 1865 the Building was vested in the Board of Works by a clause included in a supplementary Act which had otherwise concentrated on repealing the clauses of the 1854 Act relating to Marsh's Library, and the responsibility for maintenance of the building, was transferred to that Board. This was principally because the Board of the National Gallery of Ireland had made no provision to become self-sufficient. By placing the responsibility in the hands of the Board of Works the Treasury thereby avoided what might have been a constant stream of memorials seeking money for every necessary repair. This supplementary Act also granted a sum of £3,000 to be paid as 'advance rent' to the R.D.S.

The section which was intended for Marsh's Library remained unfinished for a number of years. The Board of the Gallery strenuously resisted a proposal by Commissioners appointed by the Treasury in 1863 to house the Irish Geological Collection, then located in the Museum of Irish Industry, in the vacant section of the building. The Board members had their own plans for it. For the following eighteen years, an estimate for the completion of the room was included in the Board of Works' annual estimate, but was repeatedly struck out by the Treasury until eventually, in 1881 the latter agreed to include it in the Budget. Henry Doyle, the Gallery's second director, opened the National and Historical Portrait Gallery there, having inserted a door connecting it with the Sculpture Hall. The supplementary Library on the mezzanine floor had been opened some years previously to exhibit a collection of old master drawings.

In 1891, on the 25th November, after many years of avid purchasing of works of art, Henry Doyle found it necessary to write the following memorial to the Treasury: 'I am directed to bring to the notice of the Lords Commissioners of her Majesty's Treasury the urgent need which exists for some extension of the accommodation for the works of art annually increasing as they are under the charge of this Board'. It was clear from this letter that the National Gallery, had by 1891, become an established and flourishing institution. One can see in it the germ of the later developments which were to be made by Deane in 1903 and Frank du Berry of the Board of Works in 1968, to bring the buildings to the form in which we know them today.

A SELECTION OF WORKING DRAWINGS AND DETAILS OF THE BUILDING AS CONSTRUCTED

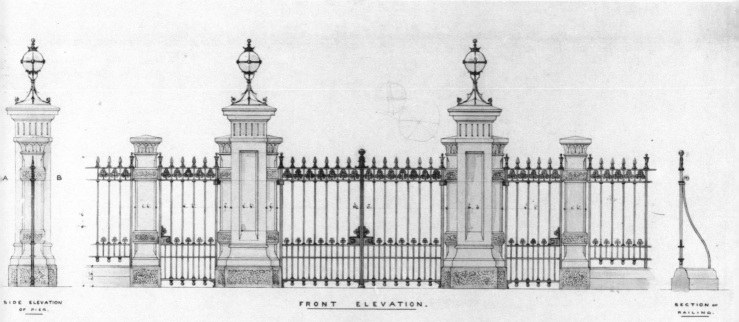

SIDE ELEVATION
OF PIER.

FRONT ELEVATION.

SECTION OF
RAILING.

51. *The south elevation. N.G.I.,*
    cat. no. 6913.

52. *The east elevation, (excluding*
    the north annex containing the
    entrance door and vestibule).
    N.G.I., cat. no. 6900.

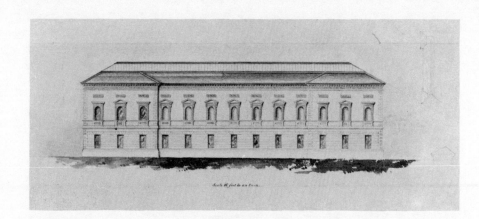

53. *The south elevation with roof, being the mirror image of the north elevation of the Natural History Museum. N.G.I., cat. no. 6914.*

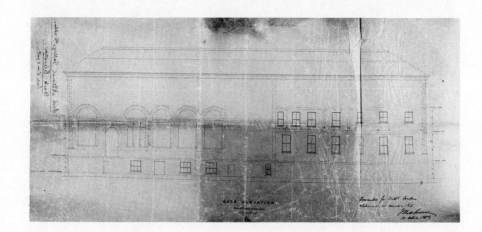

54. *The north elevation, showing the distribution of windows on the lower floors. N.G.I., cat. no. 6909.*

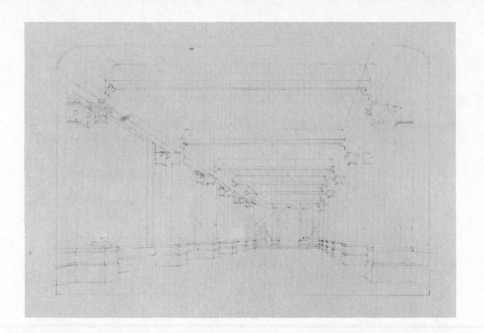

55. *A perspective of the Sculpture Hall. N.G.I., cat. no. 6967.*

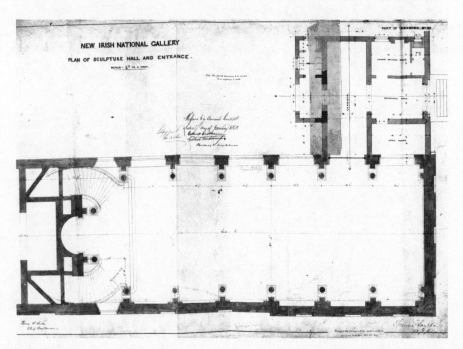

56. *A floor plan of the entrance hall and the Sculpture Hall. N.G.I., cat. no. 6947.*

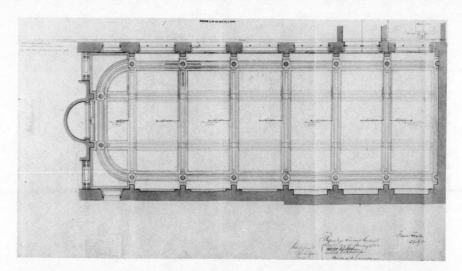

57. *Plan of the Sculpture Hall
ceiling. N.G.I., cat. no. 6983.*

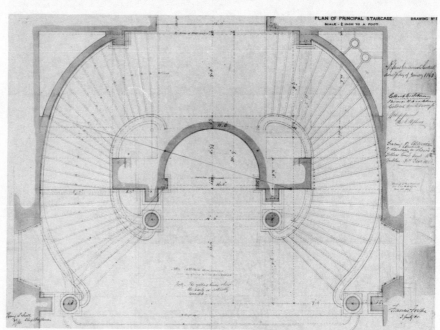

58. *Plan of the principal staircase.
N.G.I., cat. no. 6942.*

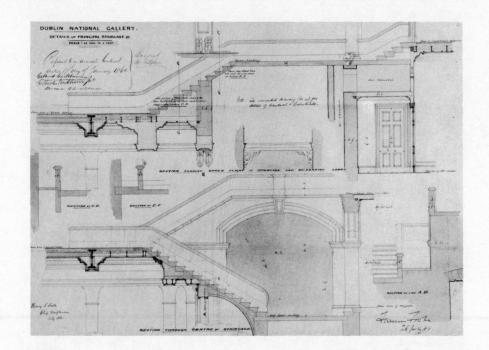

59. Details of the staircase.
N.G.I., cat. no. 6964.

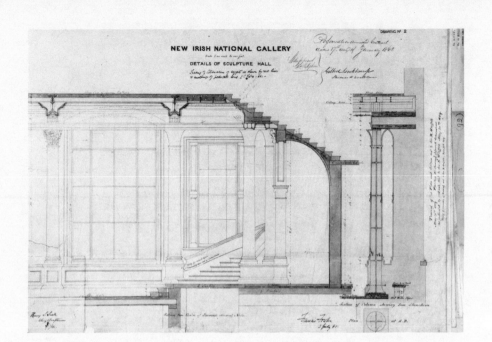

60. *Details of the staircase,*
    Sculpture Hall. N.G.I., cat.
    no. 6938.

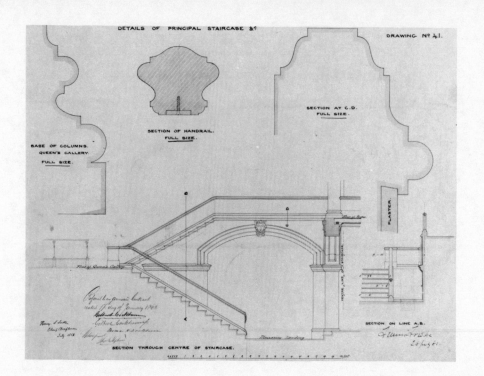

61. *Details of the staircase,
Queen's Gallery. N.G.I., cat.
no. 6979.*

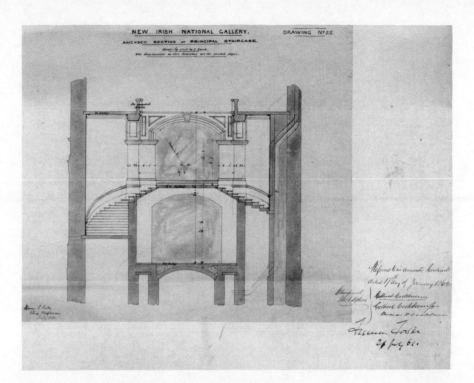

62. *A transverse section of the
staircase. N.G.I., cat. no.
6962.*

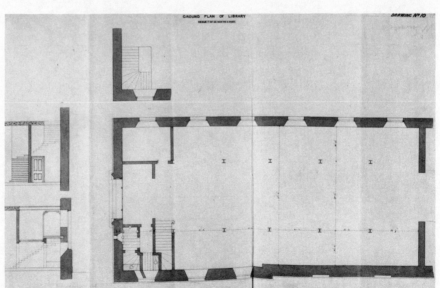

63. *Floor plan of the library.
N.G.I., cat. no. 6948.*

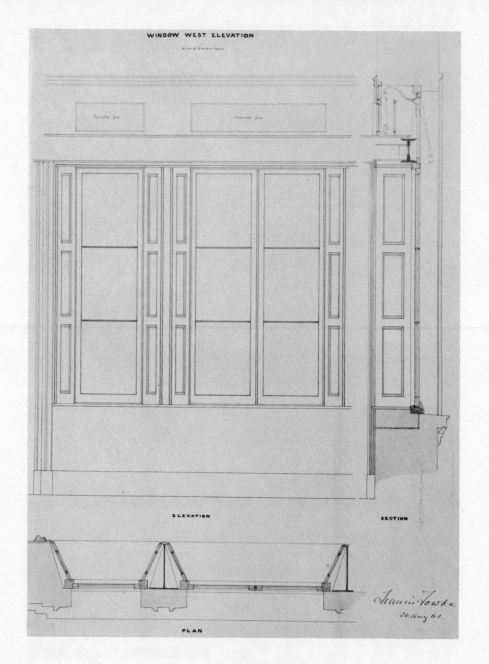

64. *Details of the west elevation window. N.G.I., cat. no. 7995.*

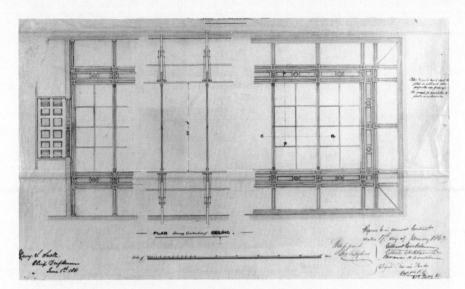

65. *Plan of the ceiling and horizontal light, Queen's Gallery. N.G.I., cat. no. 7785.*

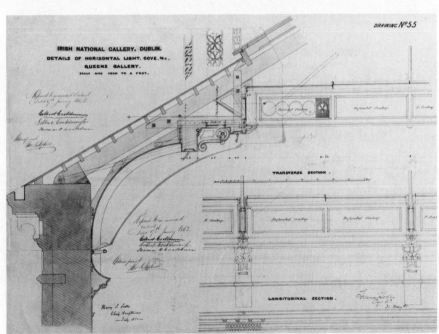

66. *Details of horizontal light, cove, etc. Queen's Gallery. N.G.I., cat. no. 7781.*

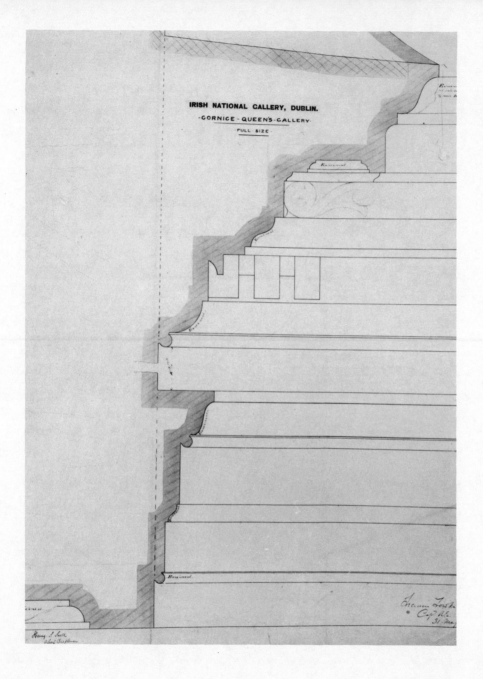

IRISH NATIONAL GALLERY, DUBLIN.

·CORNICE· QUEEN'S·GALLERY·

FULL SIZE

67. *Detail of the Queen's Gallery cornice. N.G.I., cat. no. 7991*

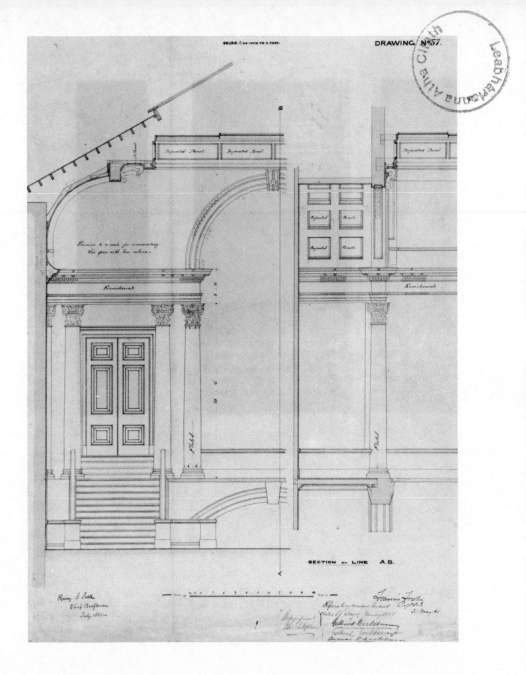

SECTION on LINE A.B.

68. *Half elevation and section of the west end of the Queen's Gallery. N.G.I., cat. no. 18,900.*

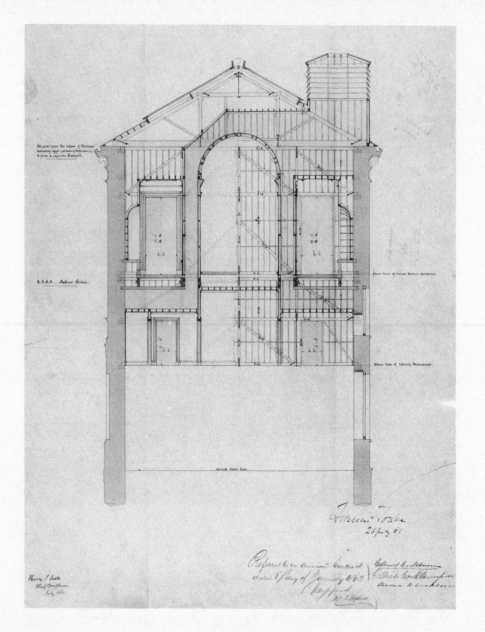

69. *A transverse section of the*
small picture galleries. N.G.I.,
cat. no. 6963.

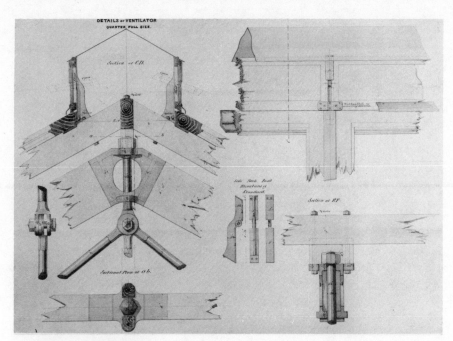

70. *Details of the roof ventilation.*
   N.G.I., cat. no. 18,057.

71. *Detail of the staircase*
   balustrade. N.G.I., cat. no.
   6954.

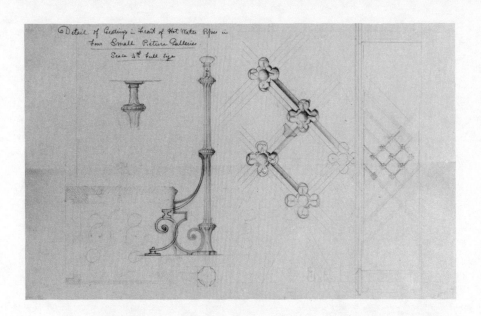

72. *Details of the iron work, small picture galleries. N.G.I., cat. no. 18,036.*

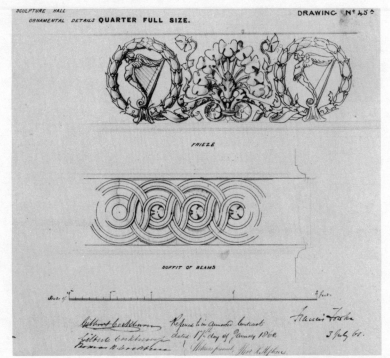

73. *Ornamental detail of the Sculpture Hall. N.G.I., cat. no. 6987.*

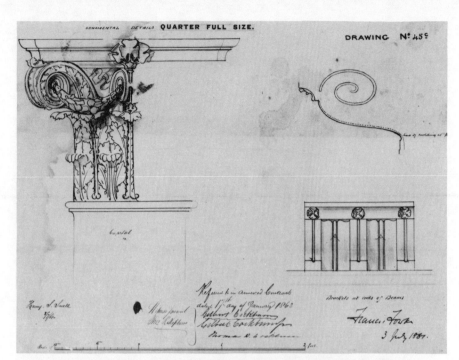

74. *Ornamental details of the*
Sculpture Hall. N.G.I., cat.
no. 6986.

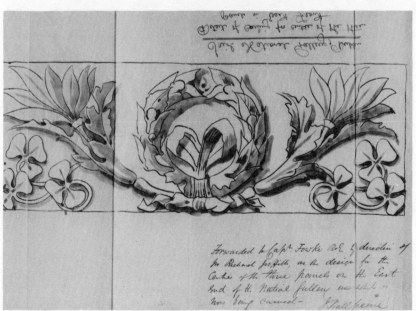

75. *A decorative panel for the east*
elevation. N.G.I., cat. no.
18,064.

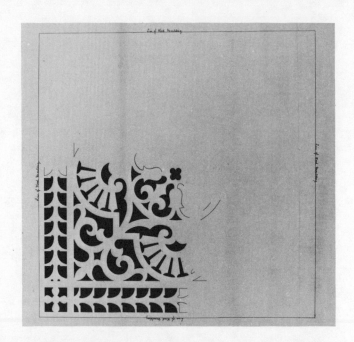

76. *Detail of a cast iron grating in the Queen's Gallery. N.G.I., cat. no. 18,021.*

77. *Detail of a cast iron grating in the Queen's Gallery. N.G.I., cat. no. 18,016.*

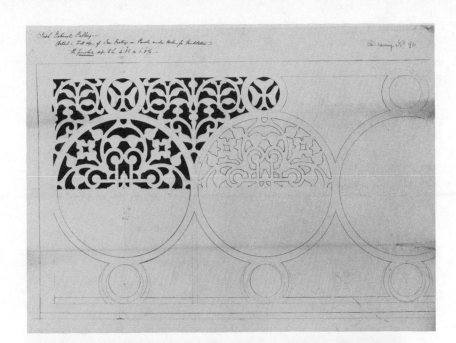

78. *Detail of iron gratings in panels under niches for ventilation. N.G.I., cat. no. 6935.*

79. *Detail of the tile paving N.G.I., cat. no. 18,038.*

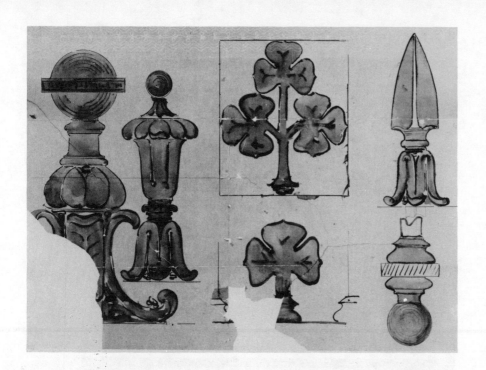

80. *Details of ornamental work of the entrance gates. N.G.I., cat. no. 6897.*

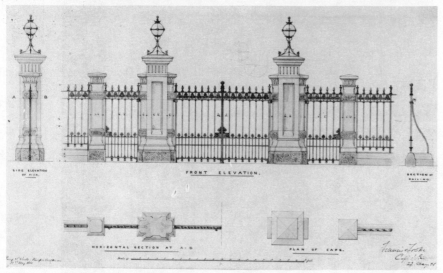

81. *Plan and elevation of the entrance gates. N.G.I., cat. no. 6893.*

92

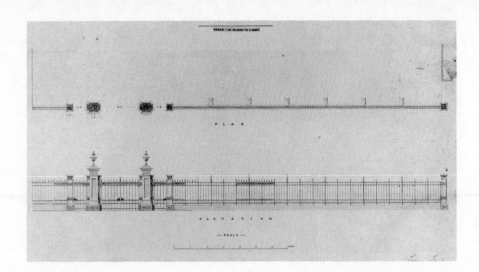

82. *Plan and elevation of the entrance gates and railings. N.G.I., cat. no. 6892.*

APPENDIX A

The Industrial Exhibition, 1853.
Source: The Irish Industrial Exhibition of 1853 by John Spoule.

(i) **Executive Committee**

George Roe, Chairman
Major Fairfield, Deputy Chairman
The Rt. Hon. the Lord Mayor
Lord Talbot de Malahide
Hon. George Handcock
Hon. John P. Vereker
Sir John Kingston James, Bart.
Sir Robert Kane
Sir Edward McDonnell
Thomas Ball
William Barker M.D.
John Barlow
John Barton
John D'Arcy
William Dargan
Lundy E. Foot
Robert Harrison M.D.
Nathaniel Hone
William Digges La Touche
John Lentaigne
J. W. Murland
John Pennefather
William Henry Porter
James Stirling
Walter Sweetman
Sir Cusac P. Roney, Secretary
John C. Deane, Assistant Secretary.

(ii) **Fine Arts Committee**

Lord Talbot de Malahide, Chairman
Sir John Kingston James, Bart.
John Barton
Robert Harrison M.D.
John Lentaigne

APPENDIX B

The Irish Institution

(i) **Those who attended informal meetings in Pigot's residence before November 1853.**
Source: The Irish Institution Minutes, 1st November 1853.

John E. Pigot
David R. Pigot
Lord Meath
Sit George Hodson
The Lord Chancellor
Lord Talbot de Malahide
'and a few other friends of artistic education in Dublin'.

(ii) **Present at the first meeting:**
1st November 1853.
Source: Irish Institution Minutes.

The Earl of Meath, in the chair
Lord Talbot de Malahide
Robert Callwell
Lord Massarene & Ferrard
J. Calvert Stronge
F. W. Brady
John Lentaigne
John Edward Pigot
George Petrie LL. D., R.H.A.
Catterson Smith R.H.A.
Walter Berwick
George F. Mulvany R.H.A.

(iii) **The first committee of the Irish Institution:**
1st November 1853
Source: Irish Institution Minutes.

President:
The Earl of Charlemont

Vice-presidents:
The Lord Chancellor
The Earl of Clancarty

William Dargan
Lord Massarene and Ferrard
The Earl of Meath
The Earl of Portarlington
Lord Rossmore
Lord Talbot de Malahide

Committee:
The Lord Chief Baron
John Barton
Mathew John Anketell
Walter Berwick
F. W. Brady
F. W. Burton R.H.A.
Robert Callwell
Martin Cregan P.R.H.A.
Rev. Charles Graves D.D., F.T.C.D.
Sir George Hodson, Bart
Thomas Hutton
John Lentaigne
The Rt. Hon. Alex MacDonnell
Alexander MacCarthy
George F. Mulvany R.H.A.
George Petrie LL.D., R.H.A.
John Edward Pigot
George Roe
Catterson Smith R.H.A.
William Stokes M.D.
J. Calvert Stronge
Rev. J. H. Todd, D.D., S.F.T.C.D.
Sir John Young, Bart. Chief Secretary

(iv) **The exhibition selection sub-committee:**
4th November 1853.
Source: Irish Institution Minutes.

Lord Talbot de Malahide
The Rt. Hon. Alexander MacDonnell
Walter Berwick
F. W. Burton R.H.A.
Martin Cregan P.R.H.A.
George F. Mulvany R.H.A.
George Petrie LL.D., R.H.A.
Catterson Smith R.H.A.

(v) **The finance sub-committee:**
4th November 1983.
Source: Irish Institution Minutes.

Lord Talbot de Malahide
George F. Mulvany R.H.A.
J. Calvert Stronge
Robert Callwell
F. W. Brady
John Edward Pigot

(vi) **The building sub-committee:**
24th November 1853
Source: Irish Institution Minutes.

Lord Talbot de Malahide
The Rt. Hon. Alexander MacDonnell
Major Thomas Aiskew Larcom
Thomas Hutton D.L.
Rev. Dr. Todd S.F.T.C.D.
Rev. Dr. Graves F.T.C.D
Walter Berwick
George Petrie LL.D., R.H.A.
F. W. Burton R.H.A.
Henry West
John Lentaigne D.L.
John Edward Pigot
George Mulvany R.H.A.
J. Calvert Stronge

(vii) **The Irish Institutions deputation to the Chancellor of the Exchequer:**
24th June 1858.
Source: The Express, 24.6.1858.

Lord Talbot de Malahide
The Earl of Clancarty
Lord Downes
The Earl of Belmore
Mr. Sullivan M.P.
Mr. Waldron M.P.
Mr. J. Hans Hamilton M.P.
Mr. William Fagan M.P.
Mr. Gregory M.P.
Mr. O. Grace M.P.
Mr. Hatchell M.P.

Mr. F. French M.P.
Mr. S. B. Millar M.P.
Sir Charles Coote Bart.
Mr. Heard M.P.
Lieut-Colonel Bernard M.P.
Mr. M'Evoy M.P.
Wm. Long, Esq.
G. A. Hamilton M.P.
Mr. Hassard M.P.
Mr. Greer M.P.
Colonel Taylor M.P.
Mr. Hone
Sir George Foster M.P.
Mr. M'Cann M.P.
Colonel Cole M.P.
Mr. L. Ellis M.P.
The Right Hon. Henry Herbert M.P.
Mr. Cogan M.P.
Mr. Clarke M.P.
Mr. Grogan M.P.
Mr. Vance M.P.
Mr. M'Mahon M.P.

APPENDIX C

The Dargan Committee:
14th July 1853.
Source The Donation of Trust 29.3.1859

The peers of Ireland who have signed the
    requisition (50)*
The representatives of Ireland who have signed
    the requisition (60)*
The Mayors of all the Corporate cities and Towns
    in Ireland*
The movers and seconders of the resolutions of
    this day (including)
The Duke of Leinster
The Rt. Hon. Francis Blackburne
John Barton, Governor of the Bank of Ireland,
Sir William Rowan Hamilton
Sir Edward McDonnell, Lord Mayor elect
John Ennis
Sir Robert Kane
Thomas McGrath, an operative trademan of
    Dublin
and: The Rt. Hon. the Lord Mayor
    John Drew Atkin
    John Barlow
    Joseph Boyce
    Robert Callwell
    Francis Codd
    Thomas Crosthwait(?)
    Joseph Cowper
    John D'Arcy
    Jeremiah Dunne
    Edward Dwyer
    Fergus Farrell
    William Fry
    Thomas M. Gresham
    Arthur Guinness
    Sir George Hodson Bart.
    George Hoyte
    Thomas Hutton

Col. Latouche
John Lentaigne
John Long
John McDonnell
James William Murland
Denis Moylan
Valentin O'Brien O'Connor, High Sheriff
John O'Connell
Thomas O'Hagan
Sir Colman Michael O'Loughlin Bart.
William Harvey Pim
James Perry
James Power
Patrick Read (e?)
John Reynolds
George Roe
Patrick Sweetman
Thomas Wilson

*unnamed

APPENDIX D

The National Gallery
The first Board of Governors and Guardians
Source: National Gallery of Ireland.

(i) **Ex Officio:**

George, Earl of Carlisle, President of the R.D.S.
Jos. D. Jackson, Senior Vice-president of the R.D.S.
Martin Cregan, President of the R.H.A.
Rev. Thomas Romney Robinson, President of the R.I.A.
Richard Griffith, Chairman of the Board of Works.

Selected by the Irish Institution for the Lord Lieutenant and the donors:

George Petrie R.H.A.
George Mulvany R.H.A.
William Brabazon, Earl of Meath
Thomas Aiskew Larcom
William Dargan
Francis William, Earl of Charlemont
The Right Hon. Maziere Brady, Lord Chancellor of Ireland
Lord Talbot de Malahide
Sir George Hodson, Bart
Robert Callwell
John Calvert Stronge
John Edward Pigot

(ii) **The Building Trustees:**

Francis William, Earl of Charlemont
Richard Griffith
George Roe
Thomas Aiskew Larcom
Thomas Hutton

(iii) **Sub-committee appointed to prepare a code of bye-laws, 13th January 1855:**

Robert Callwell
John Pigot
George Mulvany

(iv) **Building committee appointed to communicate with the Board of Works and the Building Trustees, 5th November 1855:**

George Mulvany
John Pigot
J. Calvert Stronge

APPENDIX E

Archbishop Marsh's Library, 1854.
Source: Various

Rev. Thomas Russell William Cradock, Librarian
Dr. Robert Travers, Assistant Librarian.

Board of Governors and Guardians

Lord John George Beresford, Archbishop of Armagh
Richard Whately, Archbishop of Dublin
Hon. Henry Pakenham, Dean of Christ Church
Richard Henry Dawson, Dean of St. Patrick's
Richard McDonnell, Provost of Trinity College Dublin
Sir Maziere Brady, The Lord Chancellor
David Pigot, The Lord Chief Baron
Rt. Hon. Thomas Lefroy, The Lord Chief Justice of the Queen's Bench
Rt. Hon. James Henry Monahan, The Lord Chief Justice of Common Pleas.

APPENDIX F

Royal Hibernian Academy 1854.
Source: Exhibition catalogue, 1854.

(i) **Academicians:**

Martin Cregan, President
Thomas Bridgford
Frederick W. Burton M.R.I.A.
Hugh Frazer
Charles Grey
Michael Angelo Hayes
Joseph R. Kirk A.B.
Matthew Kendrick, Keeper
George F. Mulvany, Librarian
John Skipton Mulvany
George Papworth, Professor of architecture and
    treasurer
George Petrie LL.D., M.R.I.A., secretary and trustee
Catterson Smith M.R.I.A., trustee
Thomas C. Thompson

(ii) **Associates:**

William Brocas
J. McDuff Derrick
William B. Kirk
Henry MacManus
Bernard Mulrenin
Andrew Nicholl
William Osborne
George Sharp

(iii) **Honorary members:**

Sir. R. Westmacott, R.A.
Samuel Lover
Rev. Edward Johnston, M.A., Professor of History
    to the Academy
Michael Harry Stapleton M.D., M.R.I.A.,
    Professor of Anatomy to the Academy
Richard Rothwell
Nicholas J. Crowley
Christopher Moore M.R.I.A.
Lieutenant-Colonel Colomb
Joseph Huband Smith M.R.I.A., legal advisor

APPENDIX G

Royal Dublin Society
Source: A History of the R.D.S., by H. F. Berry

Presidents:

Earl of Eglinton and Winton 1852, 1858-1859
Earl of St. Germans 1853-1855
Earl of Carlisle 1855-1858, 1859-1864

Honorary Secretaries

Lundy Edward Foot 1841-1857
Robert Harrison M.D. 1849-1858
John Francis Waller, LL. D. 1855-1861
Hon. George Handcock 1858-1861

Assistant Secretary

William Edward Steele M.P. 1852-1877

Vice Presidents

Jos. D. Jackson 1836-1858
Henry Kemmis Q.C. 1836-1857
Sir William Betham 1838-1853
Earl of Clancarty 1842-1872
John, Marquis of Ormonde, K.P. 1843-1872
Marquis of Kildare, afterwards Duke of Leinster
    1845-1874
George A. Hamilton M.P. 1847-1871
Isaac Weld 1849-1856
Lord Talbot de Malahide 1853-1883
Rt. Hon. Francis Blackburne 1856-1867
Lundy E. Foot 1857-1863

APPENDIX H

Lords Lieutenant

Montgomerie, Archibald William, thirteenth Earl
   of Eglinton 1812-1861
February 1852 – December 1852
February 1858 – June 1859

Eliot, Edward Granville, third Earl of St. Germans
   (1798-1877)
December 1852 – February 1855

Howard, George William Frederick, seventh Earl
   of Carlisle (1802-1864)
February 1855 – February 1858.

REFERENCES

Introduction

PAGE NO.	REF. NO.	
1.	1.	The National Gallery archive in relation to this study consists of the minute books from the first meeting on the 13th January 1855; the public addresses of the Board; two letter books compiled by Col. T. A. Larcom including correspondence relevant to the Gallery from 1853, newspaper cuttings, addresses of the National Gallery Board and the Acts and Bills of the National Gallery; miscellaneous correspondence not included in the Larcom letter books from 1856; c. two hundred architectural drawings of the building by Francis Fowke; nine drawings of the Fox and Barrett fire-proof floor patent used in the building; six drawings by George Mulvany; one drawing by Lanyon; one drawing by Richard Griffith and four drawings by Frederick Clarendon of the National History Museum.

Part I

PAGE NO.	REF. NO.	
3	2	*The Irish Industrial Exhibition of 1853;* a detailed catalogue of its contents edited by John Sproule. Dublin: James McGlashan, 1854. Contains a lengthy introduction outlining the background of the Exhibition.
3	3	*On the Establishment of a National Gallery of Art in Dublin, and on the means of establishing permanent exhibitions of Art in Provincial Cities generally.* Unsigned; Journal of Industrial Progress, no. 1, January 1854. Examines the development of public museums and galleries in Continental Europe and in Britain.
4	4	Archival sources on the Irish Institution in the National Gallery include minute books, 1853-1860; and correspondence addressed to Col. T. A. Larcom and to the National Gallery Board. Further information is contained in public addresses of the National Gallery Board and in the Irish Institution exhibition catalogues.
9	5	DNB (Sidney Herbert)
10	6	All the information concerning the R.D.S. involvement with the National Gallery is taken from the archive which includes copies of resolutions passed at R.D.S. committee meetings.
11	7	Information on Dargan's role in the Industrial Exhibition is contained in Sproule's introduction, op. cit. Source material in the archive includes a copy of the 'Donaton of Trust by Robert Henry Kinahan and others and the Right Honourable the Earl of Charlemont and others, 29th March 1859', which records the background of the formation of the Dargan Institute and Irish Institution meeting held in June 1854; correspondence with the National Gallery Board and with Col. T. Larcom; and a printed address to the public announcing the resignation of the Committee undated but probably January 1864.

Part II

Part III

INDEX TO THE TEXT

INDEX TO THE APPENDICES

Taken from sources as indicated in each appendix.

Massarene and Ferrard, Lord: B ii, iii
Meath, Earl of: Bi, ii, iii; Di
Millar, S. B.: B vii
Monahan, J.H.: E
Montgomerie, A.W. see Eglinton, Earl
    of
Moore, C.: F iii
Moylan, D.: C
Mulrenin, B.: F ii
Mulvany, G.F.: B ii, iii, iv, v, vi; D i, iii,
    iv; F i
Mulvany, J.S.: F i
Murland, J.W.: A i; C

Nicholl, A.: F ii

O Connell, J.: C
O Connor, V. O'B.: C
O Hagan, T.: C
O Loughlin, Sir C.M.: C
Ormonde, Marquis of: G
Osborne, W.: F ii

Pakenham, H.: E
Papworth, G.: F i
Pennefather, J.: A i
Perry, J.: C
Petrie, G.: B ii, iii, iv, vi; D i; F i
Pigot, D.R.: B i; E
Pigot, J.E.: B i, ii, iii, v, vi; D i, iii, iv
Pim, W.H.: C
Portarlington, Earl of: B iii
Porter, W.H.: A i
Power, J.: C

Read (e?), P.: C
Reynolds, J.: C
Robinson, T.R.: D i
Roe, G.: A i; B iii; C; D ii
Roney, Sir C.P.: A i
Rossmore, Lord: B iii
Rothwell, R.: F iii

St. Germans, Earl of: G; H
Sharp, G.: F ii
Smith, S.C.: B ii, iii, iv; F i
Smith, J.H.: F iii

Stapleton, M.H.: F iii
Steele, W.E.: G
Stirling, J.: A i
Stokes, W.: B iii
Stronge, J.C.: B ii, iii, v, vi; D i, iv
Sullivan, Mr.: B vii
Sweetman, P.: C
Sweetman, W.: A i

Talbot de Malahide, Lord: A i, ii; B i, ii,
    iii, iv, v, vi, vii; D i; G
Taylor, Col.: B vii
Thompson, T.C.: F i
Todd, Rev. J.H.: B iii, vi
Travers, R.: E

Vance, Mr.: B vii
Vereker, J.P.: A i

Waldron, Mr.: B vii
Waller, J.F.: G
Weld, I.: G
West, H.: B vi
Westmacott, Sir R.: F iii
Whately, R.: E
William, F. see Charlemont, Earl of
Wilson, T.: C

Young, J.: B iii.